Computerizing Production Management Systems

NHTC-NASHUA

Computerizing Production Management Systems

A practical guide for managers

J. J. Skivington

CHAPMAN AND HALL

LONDON · NEW YORK · TOKYO · MELBOURNE · MADRAS

UK	Chapman and Hall, 11 New Fetter Lane, London EC4P 4EE
USA	Van Nostrand Reinhold, 115 5th Avenue, New York NY10003
JAPAN	Chapman and Hall Japan, Thomson Publishing Japan, Hirakawacho Nemoto Building, 7F, 1–7–11 Hirakawa-cho, Chiyoda-ku, Tokyo 102
AUSTRALIA	Chapman and Hall Australia, Thomas Nelson Australia, 480 La Trobe Street, PO Box 4725, Melbourne 3000
INDIA	Chapman and Hall India, R. Sheshadri 32 Second Main Road, CIT East, Madras 600 035

First edition

© 1990 J. J. Skivington

Typeset in 10/12 Times Roman from author's disks by
Saxon Printing Ltd., Derby
Printed and bound in Great Britain by
T. J. Press (Padstow) Ltd, Padstow, Cornwall

ISBN 0 412 37720 9
    0 442 31197 4 (USA)

British Library Cataloguing in Publication Data

Skivington, J.J. (James Justin)
    Computerizing Production Management Systems:
    A Practical Guide for Managers
    1. Production management. Applications of computer systems
    I. Title
    658.5'0028'5
    ISBN 0–412–37720–9

Library of Congress Cataloging-in-Publication Data available

To my Mother

CONTENTS

INTRODUCTION

In the last ten years, the growth in the number of computerized systems used in industry has been phenomenal. Technology and systems which were once the preserve of large organizations with data processing budgets to match are now to be found, in one configuration or another, in the smallest production control office and the humblest stockroom, being used with easy familiarity in place of peg-boards and stock cards. Substantial effort and resources have been expended by manufacturing companies in an attempt to make more efficient the difficult and expensive tasks of designing, manufacturing and distributing products. Materials managers and production controllers have wrestled with the complexities of finite capacity planning, backflushing and batch traceability, and struggled to achieve what for many proved to be impossible: the implementation of an integrated manufacturing system on computer, or at the very least the running of a few key systems which would transport the organization onto a higher operational plane and once and for all do away with the fire-fighting habits of a corporate lifetime.

Yet a trip around a few dozen manufacturing organizations would soon show that a significant number of these systems, or parts of them are inoperative, with visual display units and printers lying idle under a film of dust, monuments to what might have been. In such instances the investment in hardware, software and time has long since been written off and the hopes of making a breakthrough in manufacturing administration are now but a distant memory. Comments are heard such as "I suppose we were naïve to think it was possible", "These things are all right in theory", and "It might be all right for the big boys, but you can't computerize the way we have to work here."

Just as a random sample of manufacturing units would reveal those where computerized manufacturing systems have been partially or wholly abandoned, it would also show others where the objectives had been achieved, the systems installed and working, and the financial pay-off realized. The success stories would not have been dependent on luck or on a happy coincidence of circumstances. Nor would it have been solely a matter of applying large resources to the problem. As in any human enterprise, successful outcomes are invariably the result of planned and thoughtful action, based on knowledge and determined application.

Many organizations have transformed their manufacturing sectors both operationally and financially, raising customer service to levels which previously they would have thought unattainable and achieving major savings which significantly raise the profitability of their businesses. It can be done and it has been done time and again. In some respects, the successful methods used are no different from those required by any major project. Other aspects require knowledge peculiar to computer-aided production management (CAPM) systems, not technically difficult to absorb but time-consuming to obtain and put into practice. Some companies have foundered on the rock of the 'quick fix' syndrome, the belief that the act of implementing computerized systems will of itself sweep away the problems of many years standing in their organizations – inadequate management skills, an ill-trained workforce and poor systems discipline. Dazzled by the cure-all 'high tech', they have failed to come to grips with the 'low tech' first, the need to understand and consistently apply the basic principles of manufacturing administration.

The purpose of this book is simple. It is to offer practical assistance to those manufacturing organizations who wish to choose and implement their first CAPM systems, to replace an existing one, or to discover where they have gone wrong with an implementation so that they might put it back on the road to success. It is aimed primarily at small to medium-sized companies which will be looking to off-the-shelf or 'package' software to provide them with their solutions. It is based not only on the many projects undertaken to assist companies from a wide range of manufacturing industries in their choice and implementation of such systems, or to re-start failed projects, but on many years experience gained in manufacturing and distribution companies, some of which were poorly run while others were models of efficiency. There was something to be learned from all of them.

Since this book is to be published on both sides of the Atlantic the terminology used is, as far as possible, mid-Atlantic. For instance, the American term 'inventory' has generally been preferred to its British counterpart, 'stock'; on the other hand, 'work-in-progress' (British) and 'work-in-process' (American) have been used interchangeably throughout.

CHAPTER 1

What is CAPM?

In recent years, those involved in the manufacturing industries who have taken even a passing interest in the computerization of systems have been swamped by a plethora of names and acronyms; and to date they show no signs of abating, as new systems and conglomerations of systems are devised, complete with a set of letters which have at times been ill-defined and confusing. As well as CAPM, we have others such as CAD (computer-aided design), CAPP (computer-aided process planning), CAE (computer-aided estimating, although it can also stand for computer-aided engineering), and CIM (computer integrated manufacturing). A number of these areas of activity can be linked and can also overlap, with CIM being the description for an environment in which all of these and more are integrated into one large system covering all of the key manufacturing functions.

A definition of CAPM

So, before we answer the question "Why?", let us first give a working definition of what CAPM is and where it fits in the scheme of things, albeit a scheme that is still in the making. For the purposes of this book, CAPM can be defined as:
"The use of purpose-designed, computerized systems for the administration of production management and ancillary activities". The individual areas of activity forming part of CAPM and the terminology used can vary from one suite of software programs to another, but those which are considered to be admissible are:

- Sales order processing and invoicing
- Master production scheduling
- Inventory control
- Purchase order processing
- Bills of material

- Production routeings
- Materials requirements planning (MRP)
- Process planning
- Capacity planning and scheduling
- Work-in-progress
- Costing
- Tool control.

In addition, accounts systems are increasingly seen as being part of any good CAPM system, and this can often extend to payroll programs which can be integrated with others such as costing and time and attendance. Some other systems which can either be integrated with the main ones or operated in 'stand-alone' mode are CAD and CAE. These are generally referred to as pre-production systems.

Of course, computer systems written to assist in the sometimes complex task of managing manufacturing activities are not new, and neither are most of the principles and techniques upon which they are based. Large organizations first created bespoke written programs to run on mainframe computers many years ago, with varying degrees of success. Now available, at a fraction of their former cost, are many sophisticated systems which can be run on mini-computers, networks or even on single-user personal computers (PCs). These have come to be termed 'package' programs due to their being available 'off the shelf' in a finished format – although capable of some modification – and it is with these that we will be concerned primarily as we examine the methods of choosing systems and achieving successful implementation of them.

The evolution of CAPM

A significant number of the CAPM systems now commercially available started life as the computerization of manual systems in specific companies, each set of programs bespoke-written by a data processing department or an external software house solely for the use of the organization which commissioned it, catering for its own methods of operation and planned developments. At a later stage it was recognized that, with a greater or lesser degree of adaptation, such systems could fulfil an external demand and be profitably supplied to other manufacturing organizations who were seeking ways of improving their operational efficiency and profitability. Many of these systems tended to grow piecemeal, as immediate needs were satisfied and other possibilities emerged over time. Other integrated systems were conceived and designed as a whole, with the needs of the growing market in mind, or at least to the extent that current thinking allowed. In both cases they were extended and consolidated as market demands matured, so that today we have the complex and wide-ranging manufacturing systems which are numbered in the hundreds.

Most of these suites of programs were aimed at the manufacturing industry in general. As we shall see later, the manner in which some functions are carried out in different manufacturing companies are similar, even for those production processes which are at first glance quite dissimilar. Because of this, computer products with a high degree of standardization came onto the market, offering the potential buyer the two desirable features of good functionality and relatively low price. In some industries – generally those which deviated significantly from the engineering-based methods of producing discrete parts in a 'design-machine-assemble' sequence – industry-specific package programs were developed; for example in the printing, process and shoemaking industries, and growth in this sector of the CAPM market has recently been substantial.

Just as the principles behind the 'new' philosophy of just in time (JIT) production management were in fact developed by Henry Ford and used in his automobile factories in the earlier part of this century, the basic concepts which support CAPM are not new; they have been around for hundreds if not thousands of years. There has been no quantum leap in systems concepts. It is merely the technology which has changed – the mechanics of capturing, manipulating and reporting data. And herein lies a problem. Many people within manufacturing companies, when implementing and running CAPM systems, have appeared to act on the assumption that they are working with entirely new concepts and that the old ones no longer apply, that they have at last been freed from the drudgery of data accuracy and systems discipline. *This is one of the main reasons for failure in the implementation and running of CAPM systems.* In an effort to come to grips with the 'high tech' nature of such systems, these companies fail to realize that they must first ensure that the 'low tech' aspects are correct'. Just as, in manual methods systems discipline is of paramount importance and the mere fact that production management systems are computerized is no guarantee of success in itself.

Accuracy in bills of material and stock records must be achieved and maintained, procedures for the gathering and entry of data have to be put in place and upkept, and methods of reviewing output from the computer system – whether of detailed operational data or summary management information – need to be devised and followed at all times. Similarly, there has to be a commitment by everyone involved to act upon such data as is provided and to ensure that systems users learn from experience and use the knowledge to modify manufacturing plans and make them more realistic. Such requirements are not immediately apparent when one looks at a typical CAPM system, and this phenomenon has been described as

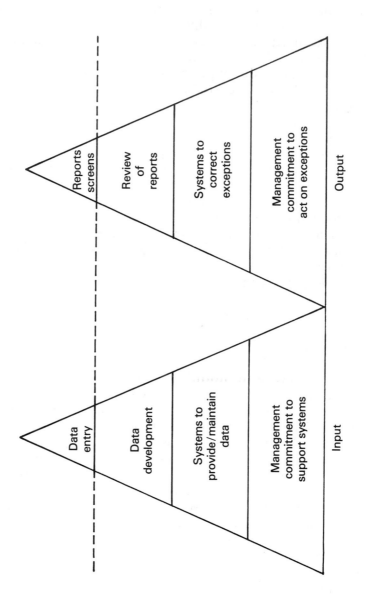

Figure 1.1 *The Iceberg Concept of CAPM*

the 'Iceberg concept' of CAPM, an illustration of which is given in Figure 1.1.

In Appendix I, Computer Systems Specification, a comprehensive list of CAPM modules or programs is given, with definitions and explanations in the Glossary where necessary. Each of these modules, when installed in a computer and used by a manufacturing company, can give significant benefits: the ability to handle large volumes of sales orders with ease and later to produce sales invoices with little subsequent data entry; and via the medium of an inventory control program, facilitating tight control on expensive raw materials without the need for the time-consuming procedures of manual systems. Yet these are only part of the benefits to be had. One of the major attractions of modern CAPM systems is that their suites of programs are integrated so that they communicate with one another, passing data back and forth or extracting it from a number of programs and using it to carry out calculations, produce reports and print documentation. The whole is greater than the sum of its parts. It is this aspect of CAPM which often brings a sense of cohesion to different departments within a manufacturing company, and indeed the chances of successfully running an integrated system without this sense of oneness are slim. It must be the aim of every organization intent on having an effective computerized manufacturing system that it should work towards total integration of all possible elements. As we shall see, this will have particular significance not only for the system chosen but for the method of choosing it.

CAPM functions and modules

So far we have looked briefly at the development of CAPM systems and some of the reasoning behind them. If we are to answer fully the question "What is CAPM?", we must look at its elements in greater detail, see the relationship between them and appreciate their individual functions within a modern manufacturing organization. Figure 1.2 shows the elements of a typical CAPM system – in this case with a materials requirements planning (MRP) module at its centre – their interrelationships and the stages in the manufacturing process which each represents. It can be seen from the illustration that the management of any manufacturing organization can be separated into four phases, namely Forecasting, Planning, Execution and Reporting. This is a somewhat simplistic approach but one which is nonetheless valid for that. Even if a modest success was all that was to be expected in a particular manufacturing company, each of these steps would have to be carried out in one form or another, and the crudest of manual systems in the smallest manufacturing unit will contain these four elements to some degree.

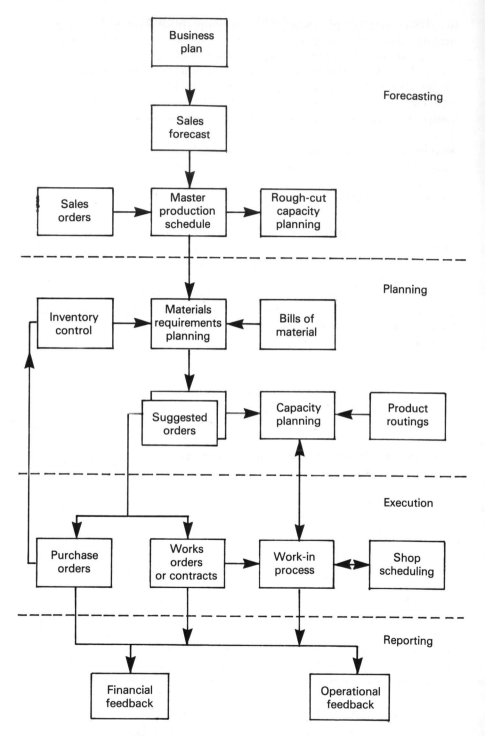

Figure 1.2 *The Elements of CAPM*

16

As in other areas of human endeavour, those engaged in manufacturing do not have a crystal ball which can show them what will occur in the weeks and months ahead. They must attempt some kind of forecast of sales levels and production rates by projecting what has happened in the past and combining it with estimates for new products or the entry into new markets. This method forms the basis of the business plan which should cover all aspects of the organization's planned activities in the chosen period, generally from one to five years. Detailed budgets are to be generated from this plan which comprises the blueprint for action in every aspect of the business, although in practice this is heavily tempered by actual conditions encountered and, most importantly, the level of sales orders received.

As well as the Business Plan and the Sales Forecast, the other key element in the Forecasting phase of CAPM systems is the master production schedule (MPS). This is the planned production or 'build' schedule, expressed in quantities and dates for each model or product, the data contained within the MPS being the main input and driving force behind a MRP program. It is comprised of firm sales orders, the sales forecast and any outstanding orders, while interfacing with and drawing data from the Rough-Cut Capacity Planning program, sometimes referred to as resource requirements planning. The primary functions of this program are to evaluate the feasibility of the plan prior to implementation and to convert the MPS into quantified demands for key resources, such as production capacity in the form of labour and machinery and storage capacity in the form of warehouse space.

With the Business Plan and forecasts providing the guiding principles and pointing the way, and the Master Production Schedule having been verified by Rough-Cut Capacity Planning, the detailed planning phase is the next to be undertaken. In Figure 1.2, MRP sits at the centre of the system model and is a key element of the planning phase. However, although many CAPM systems contain an MRP program, it is not essential nor indeed appropriate for every manufacturing company. For material control, some systems use MRP exclusively, whilst others may use JIT techniques, a combination of both, or MRP for the majority of their material needs and the more traditional 're-order point' methods for the remainder. Having said that, MRP is currently the most ubiquitous of materials planning techniques within CAPM systems and probably the one with the widest application. The choice of system or combination of systems will depend on the nature of manufacturing methods and the demands placed upon them.

Alongside the MRP module, and inseparable from it for planning and control purposes, are the Bills of Material and Inventory Control modules. By taking the Bill of Material data for each product,

17

multiplying it by the required batch quantity and exploding down through all levels – from the finished assembly to raw materials – a gross requirement for each and every item of material is calculated by the computer. If these requirements are then compared to the current and projected inventory profiles, the time-phased, net requirements for each bottom level item are given. Suggested orders are then generated in order to fulfil the predicted net requirements. The frequency with which MRP is 'run' can vary between daily and monthly occurrences, dependent upon the rate of change in material demand within each organization. In simple terms this is the function of MRP, and while the principles behind it and its method of operation are not complex, it does provide an extremely powerful tool with which to plan and control a manufacturing organization's material needs so that the maximum benefit is obtained from inventory investment.

Detailed planning of manufacturing capacity in terms of labour force and machines is another key element in the planning phase of CAPM systems. The Product Routeing module holds details of all operations and work centres through which each batch of components passes during the manufacturing cycle, and the Capacity Planning module draws upon this data and the Suggested Orders to enable it to allocate capacity, determine over- and underloads if any and re-plan when necessary.

The primary output from the MRP module after a 'run' has been completed is the Suggested Orders listing which details the quantities and order dates of all those materials required, with indications as to whether they are made-in items or to be purchased from a vendor or sub-contractor. From this point, the system moves into the Execution phase with the raising of Purchase Orders, the quantities of which are recorded as 'on order' in the Inventory Control program, and Works Orders for the manufacturing unit. A separate Purchase Order processing program keeps track of orders placed on vendors, maintains a record of prices paid and analyses data to give a measure of vendor performance in terms of price, delivery and quality. The passage of Works Orders through the production cycle is controlled through the Work-In-Process program.

One of the major problems encountered in all but the simplest of manufacturing processes is that of reconciling the demands placed upon them with their capacity to fulfil these demands within an acceptable time. We have seen how, in the Forecasting phase, the Rough-Cut Capacity Planning facility was used to determine broadly the fit between forecast demand and critical resources, and in the Planning phase this was carried out in a more detailed way using Capacity Planning with the data from MRP or from orders entered directly into the system. At the Execution stage there is a need for detailed scheduling of each batch undergoing the production process, taking into account the various operations through which they have to pass and the synchronization of other batches so that there can be optimum utilization of production capacity and delivery dates can be met. This is the function of the shopfloor scheduling module.

The primary task of the Work-In-Progress program is to keep track of each Works Order which has been launched into production and its individual batches, operation by operation if required, so that progress can be monitored and re-scheduling carried out where necessary. In addition, Work-In-Progress and related programs can also issue shopfloor documentation and record the use of resources for later analysis. The latter is a vital element in any actual costing system and most suites of CAPM programs include either standard costing, job costing or contract costing, and sometimes all three. One major advantage of such a system being integrated with the production control and Work-In-Progress program is that as set-up times, operation times and lost time are being recorded for operational and performance reasons and material usage for Inventory Control, these times and quantities are also costed and gathered against individual Works Orders or Contracts. By automatic application of pre-determined overhead rates, the total actual cost of each job, Works Order or Contract can be obtained, often alongside a comparison with the estimated or standard cost, and all of this for little extra effort. This is a prime example of the benefits of CAPM module integration and it is part of the fourth and final phase of a CAPM system's cycle, that of Reporting. It has two aspects, Operational and Financial Feedback, both of which are designed to give sufficient information on the results of the Forecasting, Planning and Execution stages to allow performance, costs and profit to be measured, and to enable modifications to be made to one or more elements of the manufacturing cycle.

The foregoing is only a very limited description of a typical CAPM system since it is not the purpose of this book to examine the detailed workings of such systems but rather to explain the equally important subject of their selection and implementation. There are a number of books and training courses available, some of which may appear under the heading of MRP while others are contained within the CIM concept. It has to be assumed that anyone seriously interested in CAPM systems will take the time and trouble to discover their capabilities and methods of operation. Without such knowledge a proper decision cannot and should not be made regarding the benefits and drawbacks of a particular application. Every bit as much as the investment in computer hardware and software and that in data preparation and in consultancy assistance, the initial investment in acquiring CAPM systems knowledge is vital and will be repaid with interest.

CHAPTER 2

Getting Started

At what point does dissatisfaction with current systems become so great that an organization begins to cast around for alternative methods and to consider the possibilities of computer-aided manufacturing (CAM)? It may simply be that the systems in daily use are in need of an overhaul, that they have become outmoded, or they are being poorly administered by staff who do not appreciate the underlying principles and are being pressured into taking shortcuts for the sake of expediency. In many organizations there are two systems: the formal one, the one which is detailed in the procedures or systems manual, what wc might call the *de jure* system; the other is the real system, the *de facto* one, comprised of a set of rules or 'understandings' evolved over the years to remedy the shortcomings of the official one. This is the system which ensures that most of the time most of the raw materials, the machines and the labour are provided, allowing the majority of production jobs to be completed within an excusable timescale. In other words: "What can we get away with? How much will the customer stand before he cancels his order and takes his business elsewhere?"

Reasons for selecting CAPM systems

In many ways, this attitude in manufacturing and sales organizations parallels that which the JIT philosophy was partly designed to combat, except that in this instance the accent is on buffer time rather than buffer stock. Both are expensive resources, luxuries which are literally cushions against the effects of inappropriate policies and inefficient methods of working. Poor results are not always the consequence of a lack of effort. Very often there is at least as much energy and ingenuity expended in keeping an old system going as would implement and run a better one. There is no doubt that people can become very efficient at running inefficient systems, and can present them as appearing, at first sight, as paragons of logic and reasonableness; yet sooner or later the need to consider change imposes itself upon management. This can be an agglomeration of many small things or one single and overwhelming reason, any or all of which can manifest themselves to the chief executive in a radically different way than they might do to a shopfloor supervisor or salesman. Some of the symptoms which may indicate the need for a systems review or feasibility study are:

1.   The organization is consistently failing to meet the price, quality or delivery demands placed upon it by its customers.
2.   The manufacturing and administrative staff using the current systems are meeting company targets, but only by exceptional personal effort.
3.   The number of administrative staff required, for example in inventory control, purchasing or production control rises in direct proportion to any expansion in business activity.
4.   Despite an acceptable level of sales, profitability is low due to excess raw materials, work-in-process or finished goods stocks.
5.   Administrative costs are unacceptably high and cannot be significantly reduced without detriment to performance.

There are of course many other symptoms which can and do manifest themselves and which are often the subject of managerial tinkering, often with little or no effect. Extra pieces of documentation and little sub-routines are designed and added to an already overburdened system, thereby bringing about the exact opposite effect to that which was intended. Bright red 'URGENT' stickers begin to appear on a few purchase orders or works orders then gradually spread until almost everything in the system is so classified. It is then that the 'VERY URGENT' stickers make an appearance, at which point the system is in danger of complete collapse. When everything is urgent, nothing is urgent. Many of these so-called temporary measures, designed to plug a leak until the system can be overhauled, are found to be still in service years later, having been incorporated into the system and presently forming a vital function within it.

It is unhappily true that the manual and computerized systems in many manufacturing organizations were never conceived as a whole but evolved over the years as various demands were placed upon them, with one sub-routine being added to another, with little regard for logic or overall effectiveness. The result was, and still is in many cases, an entanglement of unwieldy and inefficient systems which are retained because they are familiar and workable and no-one is prepared to make time for a fundamental review. "Of course, they're not perfect," you will be told, " but what is?", or "It hardly seems

21

worth all the effort to get a marginal increase in the throughput time for a works order." As we shall see, changing attitudes such as these is at least as important in a CAPM systems implementation as choosing the right software or ensuring that the project comes in under budget.

Let us take the case of a small manufacturing company whose systems are still largely manual. Sales orders are taken down by hand, typewritten and later stored in filing cabinets; the availability of raw material is checked by a clerk on the inventory cards and purchase orders are raised in triplicate by the buying office; before a works order is put onto the shopfloor, available capacity is checked through all the relevant work centres and scheduled on a planning board on the wall of the production control office or a quick check is made with the production manager; expediters keep track of batches as they move through the shop and production supervisors try to make sure that material usage, labour time and scrap are recorded for performance and costing purposes; and when the batch is finally completed, a packing note is raised manually and a copy left in the Accounts office tray to await invoicing. If you were to ask the production manager in such a company for a brief description of its systems, he or she would tell you something like that. At least, that would be the theory behind it. However, one would not need to look too far in some organizations to find that it did not quite work like that in practice. Sales orders might not always be recorded in a consistent manner, leading to ambiguity and misinterpretation; raw materials overstocking and understocking might be commonplace due to a lack of coherent policy and poor control; and batches of part-finished products could 'disappear' for days between operations on the shopfloor, pushing work-in-progress above acceptable levels.

The benefits and drawbacks

What would a CAPM system have to offer such a company? After a year of operation, what tangible benefits could be seen recorded in the balance sheet and profit and loss account, and what improvements to working methods and morale in the offices of the administrators would be in evidence? The working capital tied up in raw material and finished goods inventory might show a significant decrease; work-in-process might well be reduced by a third or more and production lead times cut by a similar amount; the production manager may be achieving greater operating efficiency and lower costs due to better utilization of finite resources. All this and more is regularly achieved with the installation of CAPM. And yet there is no doubt that in many instances a considerable amount of the benefits gained come not from the CAPM systems as such, but from the systems discipline demanded by them and an appreciation of their

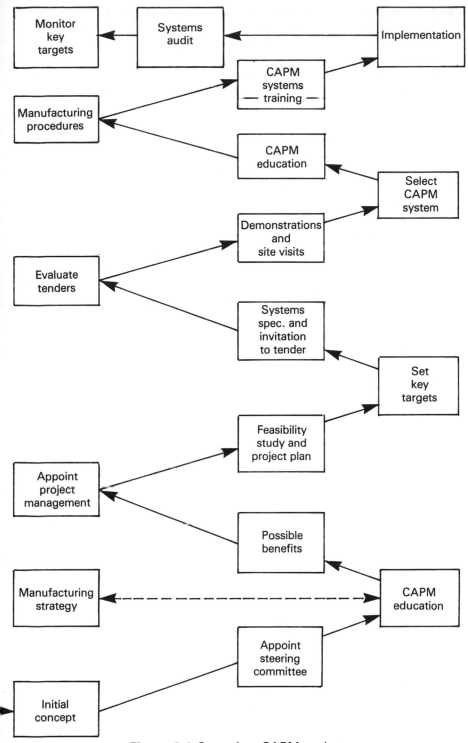

Figure 2.1 *Steps in a CAPM project*

underlying principles. In effect, major benefits often follow a change in approach and attitudes rather than simply a change in systems. Generally speaking, manufacturing administration systems are conceptually simple, although deferring to the belief that more is better, people often complicate them unnecessarily. It is the implementation and consistently efficient operation of such systems which causes the difficulties.

This brings us back to an aspect of manufacturing systems and the way in which they are seen by some organizations, first mentioned in the Introduction. When an organization is casting around for solutions to its many pressing problems it is easy to see CAPM as the answer, the 'quick fix' which will solve most of the problems in the short term, as if such systems could simply be plugged in and switched on. Nothing could be further from the truth because there is simply no point in considering CAPM if present systems (be they manual or computerized) are badly run and the users undisciplined. It will not work. The data will not be accurate enough on entry and will rapidly degrade until the output is of no use whatsoever. CAPM of itself cannot overcome poor management technique, low workforce morale and lack of organization. It can only achieve greater things by making greater demands on people: highly accurate data, greater discipline in procedures and constant feedback from both internal and external sources. It requires that the whole is based on corporate goals, a 'mission' statement if you will, which is translated into key objectives for the organization and a detailed business plan. These are things which have never been fully achieved in many organizations, have rarely been attempted, or perhaps have not even been the subject of serious consideration. But all this is required and more, for there is no sense in simply substituting ineffective computer systems for ineffective manual ones. Systems discipline is everything. If you doubt this, compare the relative ease with which software is usually implemented in an accounts department, where systems discipline is usually of a high order, with the time taken to implement an inventory management program in a badly-run stockroom.

Making out a case

Once an organization has satisfied itself that the ability and willingness are extant to adopt a disciplined approach, but that for various reasons its systems are becoming increasingly redundant, it must make out some kind of prima-facie case for CAPM before proceeding to a full-blown feasibility study. In general terms, the reasons for installing integrated CAPM systems in an organization might fall into some of the following categories, although the irreducible minimum is that there must be an increase in profitability and/or sales revenue:

- a reduction in administrative costs
- a reduction in the lead time between taking a sales order and delivering the finished product to the customer
- better utilization of resources leading to lower manufacturing costs
- greater flexibility in the production response to sales
- the ability to gather accurately the actual costs incurred in manufacturing
- an improvement in the price/quality configuration of finished products.

These would not only apply to, and be achieveable with, a complete and integrated CAPM system, but to a greater or lesser extent by implementing single modules either in 'stand-alone' mode or a number of linked ones, such as Purchasing and Inventory Control.

Choosing a consultant

Before looking at the objectives and methods involved in a feasibility study, we must first consider who is going to carry out the study, write the systems specification and assist with the implementation, always assuming that the study shows provable benefits to be derived from CAPM. In practice this often means deciding whether or not you should employ an external consultant. Like most other decisions of this nature, this one should be based on an objective evaluation of key factors, and the possibility not simply dismissed out of hand as being expensive and unnecessary.

Acquiring a good consultant could well make the difference between success and failure in a project which is going to consume a large amount of the organization's resources and bring dramatic changes to the way in which it operates. Two questions must therefore be answered: How does one decide whether or not to use a consultant?, and What kind of consultant is needed?.

Let us first look at some of the wrong reasons for deciding to use a consultant or not:

Using a consultant

- nobody within the organization wants to be responsible if the project goes wrong
- the chief executive officer (CEO) knows a good man who is cheap
- the capital requisition might not be passed if you don't
- without investigation, the assumption is made that there is inadequate skill or experience within the organization.

Not using a consultant
- they are too expensive and contribute little
- without investigation, the assumption is made that there is adequate skill and experience within the organization
- choosing the 'right' systems will ensure a trouble-free implementation
- the systems vendor will handle all aspects of the implementation
- systems are so 'user-friendly' nowadays that they can easily be implemented by the intelligent layman.

From the outset, the potential project should be approached in a businesslike manner with the seriousness that such a major undertaking deserves. There is no place here for the amateur or the manager who 'knows a bit about computers'. And strangely enough, as we are primarily concerned here with what are known as 'package' programs or 'off-the-shelf' systems, there is often little place for an organization's data processing staff to mastermind the process. This is because, being used to bespoke or heavily-adapted software, they often have little or no knowledge of package systems. Perhaps more importantly, given that one of the attractions of these programs over the bespoke-written variety is that they rarely need data processing staff to run them, such people have a vested interest in retaining those systems which ensure them steady analysis, programming and maintenance work. The strongest resistance to the implementation of such systems as a replacement for bespoke ones, often comes from an organization's computer staff. In any case, even if there was no likelihood of staff reductions the new systems would almost certainly decentralize the computer functions away from the data processing department and into the hands of the user departments. It has been noticeable during the last few years that with the advent of 'user-friendly' systems and the growth of computer literacy among general staff, data processing personnel in the small to medium-sized companies have become something of a dying breed. Naturally, assumptions and uninformed judgements should not be made about the ability of data processing staff to carry out a CAPM project since a wealth of relevant experience may reside there. Each case should be judged on its merits.

How then to choose a consultant? Before embarking on the search for the appropriate person it is best if you briefly write down what that person will be required to do. This could include:

- carrying out a feasibility study company-wide for specified departments or functions
- formally presenting the findings to the board of directors
- writing a computer systems specification and provide the names of potential vendors
- writing and submitting an invitation to tender

- assessing the tenders received, making recommendations and assisting in the final selection
- drawing up a project plan and assisting in the implementation of all the CAPM modules.

At some point this list, or part of it, can be expanded to include details of the specific programs your company wishes to install, the budget figure which has been allocated and the time-scale which has been allowed for the whole project and the individual elements within it. If extended to two or three pages it would serve as a brief for any consultancy wishing to tender for the job, always a useful tool to ensure that each contender is quoting for the same amount and quality of work.

Unfortunately there are no legal requirements for the person who chooses to call him or herself a consultant, whether of the computer, management or manufacturing variety. In recent years the term has sadly been abused by those who wish to give a degree of authority and prestige to a mundane position, as in 'sales consultant', or to imply the possession of experience and skills by a person who does not really have them. If a consultant is to be used, the type required for the selection and implementation of CAPM systems is preferably a management consultant with good CAPM and manufacturing experience. There is good reasoning behind this. The selection and implementation of CAPM systems is not so much a computer project as a 'people' project and requires the wide-ranging skills of the management consultant. He must be more psychologist than technologist because such an undertaking is to do with the management of change, and changing their attitudes and working methods is what most people least like to do.

Here are some points to bear in mind when considering the question of consultancy assistance with a CAPM project:

1. Do ensure that the consultancy you choose is independent. That is, they do not sell directly or have a corporate family relationship with other companies who sell computer hardware or software. What you want is an objective feasibility study and selection exercise, not a foregone conclusion where you end up with their company's products whatever your requirements. Beware of those who appear to be trying to sell you something, whether it be a concept such as MRP, JIT, etc, or a specific product, even before they have been assigned the job and conducted the feasibility study.

2. Do consider a number of consultancies unless you have used one successfully before and are confident that they are expert in CAPM. Don't assume that the biggest are the best: this is not always the case. Beware of those firms whose consultants all appear to be in their twenties. Many of them recruit straight from university, and while these young people may be brimming over with the latest theories

and techniques, their understanding and experience in a real-life manufacturing situation is open to question.

3. Do make efforts to engage the right consultant for your organization's needs. This means making sure that he or she has had sufficient experience in computer systems selection and implementation work in a similar environment to yours and that the personality of the chosen consultant will accord with the corporate personality and be compatible with those whom he or she will be required to work alongside over a lengthy period of time. This can only be achieved by interviewing the potential consultant and obtaining details of his or her previous assignments.

4. Do obtain a quotation not only for the first part, the feasibility study, but also for the much longer and more costly implementation phase. Some consultancies will offer to do a number of days or even weeks work at a reduced price, or free in some instances. This is merely a 'loss leader', the cost of which will be recouped in the main project for which you will surely sign up if the first part is free and competently executed. The proposal or terms of reference from the consultancy should lay out in detail what the objectives of the project are, what work the consultancy will carry out and what they will achieve.

5. Don't decide to go it alone simply because consultancy fees look very expensive. If you haven't got the skills in the organization, you either take a person onto the payroll full-time (and what happens when the project is completed?), or you engage a consultant. You should be prepared for the consultancy fees to be in excess of 20 per cent of the combined hardware and software price, and an allowance for this should be made in the financial justification which we will consider later. Using a consultancy may appear to be expensive but it will in most instances be cheaper than doing without their expert knowledge.

Some organizations seem reluctant to use management consultants, partly because of the cost and also because they are fearful that once a consultancy gets its foot in the door, so to speak, it will be difficult to dislodge. There are certainly a few consultancies that take an aggressive approach to sales but the story of the leech-like consultant is largely a myth which has been given credence by those organizations who did not clearly specify what they required, or were so poorly run that the consultants continued to find faults in the client organization and recommended that they be rectified. Other companies regard the use of consultants as an admission of inadequacy by the management and therefore shy away from it. Of course, a consultant is not a substitute manager (except in those cases where that is specified by the client); he or she is generally called in to do a specific job, just like an electrician or a plumber. If your organization is big enough to employ internal consultants of the right type, one or more of them should be used. If not, you should call in external people to do a specific job. Unless you wish to retain a consultant on a daily basis because you cannot tell at the outset what the duration or frequency of the work will be, you should have the consultancy quote you for a specific job at a fixed price. You may be told how many man-days will be needed, but if you are quoted for a project to be carried out, clearly the implication is that the consultants are responsible for completing the job whether or not they have to put in more time at their expense. If however it can be clearly demonstrated that the delay was outside their control, and more often than not this is the case, then the client company would be expected to pay for the extra time required.

CHAPTER 3

The Feasibility Study

Having expended time and effort in learning the capabilities and potential benefits of integrated CAPM systems, in the first flush of enthusiasm it is all too easy for someone to suggest placing an immediate order, especially in the knowledge that every month's delay could be a month's savings lost. Already the benefits and cost-savings are glaringly obvious and overwhelmingly convincing, the costs and possible disruption minimal. So much so that even the accountant agrees that CAPM sounds like a good idea! There is no argument in favour of time-wasting and every argument against it. After all, decisiveness is the hallmark of good management and while detail is not unimportant, the larger picture is what matters.

Of course, this is the very time at which the potential purchaser of a CAPM system must curb his or her understandable enthusiasm and consider the long-term view. Often this fails to happen, especially where the management of the company has no previous experience of integrated CAPM systems and is considerably impressed by their first exposure to them. Someone takes a few names from the 'Computer systems' section of the telephone directory and is thus well on the way to acquiring a CAPM system of some kind or other. Or the CEO might make the decision on his own. A few years ago, the chairman of a very large food company on a trip to California saw an advertisement on television for a computerized production management system. On returning home he contacted the local agent for this system, had him come out to demonstrate it and signed up soon afterwards, thereby committing two manufacturing plants to hardware and software inappropriate to their needs and without any defensible cost-justification.

Incidents of this type are not unusual, where a system is acquired by default. For example, an accounts system is installed and running before anyone considers the needs of the manufacturing functions within the company. The result is that in order not to have to throw out the hardware and software and start again, the only manufacturing system which can be used is the one which will run on the existing hardware and completely interface with the financial software, regardless of the needs of the company and the functionality of the software. Numerous companies have ended up with the wrong suite of manufacturing programs because of their pre-emption by accounting systems. It has not only been costly in financial terms but, because the systems have been inadequate or just plain wrong for their applications, they have alienated many of the workforce and given them a jaundiced view of all CAPM systems. In order to obviate such costly actions it is essential that a proper feasibility study is carried out, and that is the subject which we now consider.

The scope of the study

Before the investigations proper are begun, it is important that the scope of the study is decided and formally recorded, as indeed all aspects of the project should be. This will depend on a number of factors, and would fall into one of the following categories:

- a complete review of all manufacturing, material and financial control systems, to replace existing manual ones
- a complete review of all manufacturing, material and financial control systems, to replace existing computerized ones
- a review of selected systems such as material control, with a view to replacing them
- an investigation as to the feasibility of implementing a stand-alone program in manufacturing, such as inventory control.

Considerable thought should be given to the various possibilities at this stage, as it is much easier, if a little more expensive, to carry out a computer feasibility study on all aspects of the business and later drop those which prove irrelevant, than it is to review only those systems which urgently need replacing and discover later that other areas also require investigation. As we shall see, one of the objects of a feasibility study is to attempt a look forward, to give an estimate of future systems requirements. There is no point in going for the easy option at this stage because you know what your immediate needs are, and it might be difficult and dangerous to speculate about where the organization will be in five years time. It is those organizations with vision and the ability to plan ahead which will reap the benefits, while other companies are counting the cost of throwing out their three-year-old hardware and software, or having expensive software re-writes carried out because they now need features and functionality which they did not even consider at the time of systems purchase.

Appointing a steering committee

It is at this point that a steering committee should be set up, initially to give its opinion on which areas will be investigated. This subject will be treated fully in a subsequent chapter but it is enough to say here that any such committee should be representative of those functions which are to be considered for computerization, since it's those people who have the greatest knowledge of the present systems and can advise the CEO accordingly. It is the opinion of some CAPM consultants that a degree of education in the subject is desirable for all senior management at this early stage so that informed decisions can be made. Others consider that this can wait until a decision has been taken in principle to acquire a CAPM system. Of course, it is necessary that management have a good appreciation of CAPM systems capabilities, and some members of staff may already have experience in this field. But it is a mistake for most managers to spend time and effort on it, as it may turn out to be wasted if the decision goes against implementation; better that one person is chosen to find out what CAPM might have to offer the organization and then brief his or her colleagues.

What is required of a computer feasibility study is that an investigation of the current systems is carried out in order to determine what they are supposed to do, how well they do it and whether improvements can be made in a cost-effective manner with the use of CAPM systems. It is no part of a feasibility study to apportion blame for the wrongs of the past, although it is legitimate that it briefly explains what has gone before as an aid to understanding the present status of the systems. The study should be objective and thorough – hence the strong case to be made for using an external consultant – but should not go into voluminous detail with flowcharts showing the route of every piece of documentation in the organization and lists of duties and responsibilities for each person from the CEO to the stock clerk. Only those aspects germane to the case need be included in the report, the strengths and weaknesses of individual systems and the likely remedies. Be prepared for some shocks. The way that senior management believe their systems work is not always the way that they operate in practice, and they may find themselves disputing the investigator's version of events. If he or she has been halfway thorough in his or her researches, he or she is almost certainly going to be correct.

The reasons for this disappointing state of affairs is simple. Those people within the organization who use the manufacturing systems irregularly, if at all, have a theoretical notion of how they work. Perhaps they were involved in setting them up in the first place, but nothing stays the same for very long without constant vigilance, and manufacturing systems are no exception. Circumstances change and people adapt and bend the systems to suit; they take short-cuts and devise their own little sub-routines because they don't like the official ones or find them cumbersome to operate. In short, they improve them, if only within their own narrow sphere of interest and knowledge and these changes largely go unrecorded, until such times as someone carries out a detailed investigation. Considering the importance of systems in a manufacturing organization – efficient or not, they keep the business running – it is surprising how little attention is generally given to them until their weaknesses provoke a crisis.

Who should execute the study?

If you wish to use one or more persons from within your organization to conduct the feasibility study (and possibly the subsequent implementation) then who should it be? The following guidelines should assist in choosing an appropriate person:

1. Someone who can be seconded to the task full-time and temporarily relinquish his or her normal duties and responsibilities.
2. A person with ability and previous experience in conducting objective investigations and writing succinct reports.
3. Someone who has the confidence of both management and shopfloor personnel and has not been involved in any sectarian or inter-departmental strife. (Although CAPM systems are not 'political' to the same degree as some other aspects of corporate life, any sign of favouritism or bias in their acquisition by different departments can arouse strong feelings.)
4. Preferably, the person chosen should be the one who is most likely to be the project leader and who is going to implement the chosen systems.
5. It should not be assumed that someone from the data processing department would be the natural choice. Although there will be some exposure to hardware and software jargon during the project there will be no need for the person to know the technicalities of computing. If anything, such knowledge could be a distraction from the main task of discovering the strengths and weaknesses of the present systems, exploring CAPM alternatives and conducting a cost/benefit analysis. Strange as it may appear, as we are considering package programs, this process is more about systems than it is about computers.

Percolation of CAPM intentions

Having established the scope of the feasibility study – that is the areas within the organization which are to be investigated and those functions which are not currently carried out but may be undertaken

33

in the future – and having chosen the person or persons to conduct the study, every person in the company who could possibly have an interest in it should be informed. As in most corporate matters, it is better to over- than under-inform staff. Apart from those exceptional circumstances where commercial considerations and matters of personal confidentiality are paramount, management should not be conducted on a 'need to know' basis, as is so often the case, although it must be said that ill-informed staff are more often the result of poor management practices than deliberate secrecy. It is not unknown for a management consultant to arrive at a company to start an assignment and find that the only person who knows anything about the project is the CEO who engaged him. In one particular case the consultant was then abandoned to find his own way around the company, discover the functions of key personnel, and explain why he was there. Needless to say, this was hardly conducive to openness and co-operation from the bewildered staff. Informing, educating and training company personnel will be a constant theme throughout this book, and the process should start at the outset right after a decision has been made to take the first step on the CAPM route.

The method to be used

There are a number of approaches which can be taken to a CAPM feasibility study, ranging from the spurious one where the investigator simply asks each departmental head for a 'wish list' of features and functions, to those highly structured methods which are justifiable only for expensive bespoke systems to run on mainframe computers. What is needed for the kind of systems we are concerned with here is something in between these two extremes, a methodology which will cover all aspects of the manufacturing systems through the expenditure of reasonable effort within a limited time. Just as you do not have to specify to the salesman that the car you buy must have some kind of steering mechanism and a transparent windscreen, there are a number of things which are given about CAPM programs. Therefore you will be primarily concerned with discovering and specifying key aspects of the present and required systems, not with designing a new one from first principles.

Manufacturing systems feasibility (MSF)

A simple such methodology is manufacturing systems feasibility (MSF) which is primarily aimed at those organizations seeking a complete CAPM system or a substantial part of one, whether or not that organization already has computerized systems in operation. The MSF method consists of five steps, namely:

Phase One: Investigate the present systems and determine their objectives, main methods and features.

Phase Two: Critically examine the resulting data, classify the levels of achievement and shortfall.

Phase Three: Where necessary, devise new system outline and check CAPM for required features.

Phase Four: Carry out an initial cost/benefit analysis.

Phase Five: Draw up a systems specification, with features and weightings.

In practice, part of the second phase will often take place simultaneously with Phase One, where systems users and managers will give the investigator details of how the current systems operate and their opinions as to what is required. However, it is likely that the people being interviewed during the investigation, such as the inventory controller, production planner or even the manufacturing manager, do not have experience of CAPM and no clear idea of what it can provide. This is where the knowledge of the person conducting the project is invaluable. He or she must be able to ask the right questions, interpret the answers, and construct a model of the optimum system, drawn from prior knowledge of CAPM systems and their capabilities. Otherwise a systems specification for submission to potential suppliers may be written containing requirements which range from the naïve to the impossible. This is a further argument in favour of having an external consultant carry out the project, although it need not be a conclusive one.

For the purposes of illustration we will assume that your organization, let's call it XYZ Co, wishes to test the feasibility of implementing a complete and integrated CAPM system, from sales order processing through material and production control to despatch and invoicing. This will be one which is built around a MRP system because the management of XYZ hopes initially to gain major benefits in material control and then use this as a springboard into the application of the JIT philosophy.

Phase One: Investigate the present systems and determine their objectives, main methods and features

To commence Phase One you should list all those functions within the company whose systems will need investigation, even if they themselves are not subjects for possible CAPM consideration. It is important to give some time to the examination of those systems which interface with the ones being investigated, as the former may be a determining factor in the methods of operation and configurations of the latter. For example, it might be important to understand the effects of a company's design department systems when investigating the creation and use of bills of material. In the case of XYZ Co, the following might be the areas of interest:

- Sales
- Drawing office and process planning
- Stores
- Inventory control
- Purchasing
- Production planning
- Shopfloor control
- Costing

Having determined the areas and functions to be examined, the investigation proper should commence. It is necessary to achieve a full understanding of the activity in each area and the reasons for it, whether legitimate or not. Reasons given for the nature and manner of what is done are not always easy to assess, as staff are not necessarily properly instructed and may only have a vague idea about the relationship to other departments and the implications of their actions. Digging out the facts so that a true picture of present methods and possible CAPM requirements can be formed is often the most difficult part of the feasibility study.

The investigation will normally be carried out using three techniques:

Interviewing key personnel within each area of interest, including senior management and the chief executive if necessary. The objective here is to discover the true nature of the business, the policies which have been formulated to administer it and to determine how present manufacturing systems operate. It is equally important to gather opinion on the shortcomings of the systems *and their operational and financial implications,* as on the features which users would like to see incorporated in any new system. It must be remembered that when asked what they do and how they accomplish it, people do not usually give the information in the manner in which the investigator wishes to understand and record it. They relate procedures and tasks out of sequence because some are more important to them than others, they make assumptions about the interviewer's knowledge, and they miss out parts of the system which may be crucial to a full understanding of it. As in any task of detection it is the investigator's job to uncover the facts by asking the correct questions.

Examining documentation in order to determine the flow of information, its form and content. It is not considered necessary for the acquisition of package CAPM programs that extensive flowcharting of the present system is carried out, although an overview of data movements can often help to clarify what might be a complex system. As in the interviewing process, the investigator must be prepared to receive plausible but misleading reasons as to why so many documents with so many copies are sent to so many people. There may well be good reasons as to why certain methods were initiated, but they are often lost in the mists of time and no one has had either the time or inclination to discover and evaluate them.

Observation of working methods, both in administration centres such as production and material control, and in the manufacturing areas. This latter area may be of special importance if, for example, it is intended that a shopfloor data collection system is installed at some stage. However, observational activities are likely to form only a minor part of the investigator's activities.

Phase Two: **Critically examine the resultant data, classify the levels of achievement and shortfall**

When the investigation of company objectives, policies and present systems has been completed, they must then be critically examined by the investigator, both in the light of opinions given by those who administer them, and with the aid of his or her own experience and knowledge. There must be some kind of systems model known or constructed, if only in the mind of the investigator, a 'best practice' yardstick which can be used to measure the efficiency and effectiveness of current methods so that strengths and weaknesses can be made clear.

The primary aim of this phase is to make an objective assessment of the suitability of purpose of the current systems, because this will be one of the main determining factors in whether or not new CAPM systems are required. When faced with a wide-ranging and complex series of interfacing sub-systems (eg for setting up and maintaining bills of material, production routings, actual cost gathering) it is not easy to form a clear opinion as to their overall worth. One can usually see whether a specific sub-routine achieves its objective, by giving advance notice of due deliveries from vendors, for example, or ensuring that individual batches of raw material are traceable throughout the manufacturing process. To make an assessment for each system such as purchasing, stock control or capacity planning, and also for the complete manufacturing system within an organization is substantially more difficult. The answer must be to evaluate features and elements of functionality in the present system one by one and then 're-assemble' them to arrive at an assessment of the whole.

Phase Three: **Where necessary, devise new systems outline and check CAPM for required features**

When intending to seek out your new CAPM system from among the ranks of the off-the-shelf or package programs, it is not necessary to give detailed descriptions and flowcharts for each program that you wish to implement. One of the strengths of these systems is that such things are unnecessary. The report generator facility found in many CAPM and accounts systems is a good example. In bespoke-written systems and in some less sophisticated package programs, the reports required from a particular program, let's say sales order processing, would have to be specified in detail, eg monthly sales by product group, region by region; monthly sales by product group by customer type. With a report generator, provided the data is on file in an acceptable format and is accessible, the sytems users can pull it out in almost any configuration they care to name. Nevertheless, not all systems have a report generator and if this is the case it's as well to specify the reports required and their frequency.

The systems outline which should be drawn up is for the use of the investigator or project team in clarifying what is required of the new systems, if available. When the investigator has scant knowledge of CAPM systems capabilities the process of determining requirements will be iterative, where the features of CAPM systems will be looked at and the company's requirements modified in the light of what is available. This of course is something of a trial and error process and may take some time. If a consultant has been engaged to carry out the project, he or she would be expected not only to know these things as a matter of course but to be up-to-date on what is available in the market place. Hour for hour, a consultant's time is much more expensive than that of an unskilled person but because of their knowledge and experience, consultants need much less time to accomplish the same thing. In the long run, it may well be cheaper to employ a consultant.

Phase Four: Carry out a cost/benefit analysis

In order for company executives to make a rational decision on whether or not a CAPM system should be purchased and implemented, they must have before them an estimate of the *financial* costs and benefits, as well as an estimate of the cost of not implementing such systems. It is surprising the number of companies who do not look at this latter aspect, and there are those who do not carry out any justification exercise at all, presumably on the basis that computerized systems, as opposed to manual ones, are intrinsically 'a good thing'. At the very least, such an approach amounts to bad management of corporate resources and should never be condoned under any circumstances. The selection and implementation of CAPM systems takes time, money, effort and determination in large quantities and it is unacceptable to ask people to sanction or give these without making out a good case for their being cost-effective. If there is any doubt as to the necessity for going into all this detail on cost/benefit analysis, or any other part of the feasibility study, and the temptation is to do a quick job on the project you might ask yourself what your answer will be in two years time when the implementation has been disastrous and a superior asks, "Why did you choose this system?"

You will notice that there is a reference above to *financial* costs and benefits. This is because everything in the way of a cost or a benefit to the organization should be quantified in monetary terms. If it cannot be so quantified then it should not be included in the justification. This is no place to discuss the inflexibility of current accounting practice but as long as the reckoning in industrial and commercial companies is carried out in the way that it is, one cannot balance quantified costs with unquantified benefits, such as "reduced clerical work" or "higher quality products". Such statements beg the questions "How much reduction in paperwork and at what cost saving?", and "What percentage of scrap, re-work and warranty claim reduction?" Of course, these estimates are never easy to calculate. They are a matter of conjecture; detailed cost data may be needed in order to calculate them. But the task should not be shirked. Not only are precise figures more convincing than vague statements which are no more than pious hopes, they will serve as objectives which must be attained to make the project worthwhile.

Phase Five: **Draw up a systems specification with features and weightings**

The objective of drawing up a CAPM systems specification is to be able to present an invitation to tender to potential suppliers so that they can all respond to the same document and in a similar enough manner to make their tenders comparable. Even so their replies to the same document can often be radically different. Using the MSF technique, the data gathered during the investigation stage is used to determine the features and functions required of the proposed systems. These can then be classified in one of three ways: necessary, desirable and marginal, and given values relative to their worth so that any potential software package can be evaluated and a precise degree of fit calculated.

At this point you may be wondering why, so far, there has been no mention made of computer hardware. This is mainly because of the golden rule of CAPM systems selection: "Always select the software first and then find the hardware to support it". There is no point in starting the other way round, unless the organization is already in possession of hardware which, for financial or political reasons must be used. It has been said that, with some exceptions and provided that you purchase quality equipment, hardware is of much less importance than software, although of course the hardware manufacturers and suppliers would deny this. Your company might need a mainframe or a minicomputer, or choose to set up a networked system, but in the final analysis, it's the software which provides the necessary functionality. After all, what's the point of having an elegant and superfast computer which will not support material traceability and contract costing programs when these two features are essential for running your business? Far too many companies in manufacturing have been sold a computer by hardware salesmen, 'box-shifters' as they are sometimes known, only to find that it will not run the required software and they have to settle for systems which are second or third best. Then, for the sake of appearances, the inappropriate hardware and software have to be used for a decent period of time. In fact not only used but stoutly defended as the best possible system for the needs of the organization. Having said this, if your company is part of a group, and especially an international one, it is always worthwhile checking to see if there is a group policy on the purchasing of hardware. Some organizations have gone through the process of conducting a feasibility study, choosing potential vendors, receiving and vetting tenders and making a final selection, only to have someone at group headquarters inform them that all hardware must be purchased from a designated vendor who was not on the shortlist.

The investigation of present systems and specification of requirements must not be skimped, as it is upon these two phases that the future systems will be built. In the specification you do not need to go to the level of detail demanded by a bespoke-written system, but the functionality required from the programs and their interrelationships must be clearly stated. Not only does this lay down your precise requirements, with the minimum of room for misinterpretation by the vendor, but it should also elicit a written point-by-point response upon which systems selection will be based. This document can also be very useful at a later stage if there are problems with the software performing to specification.

CHAPTER 4

The Investigation: Key Questions for each Function

The feasibility study can be carried out by various methods, although it is preferable if it follows the manufacturing sequence; that is, starting at sales and going through production to despatch. This will help the investigator to understand each sub-system and set of procedures because he or she will know what has gone before, the origin of documentation and the feedback required. Let us now look in some detail at each activity which we outlined above for the XYZ Co. Not all of the functions within each department are to be computerized, and in any event they would not all fall within the scope of this book. Yet most of them will have to be considered, however briefly, as having implications for those parts of the systems with which we are concerned.

Sales

The functions carried out by the Sales Department can vary greatly from one organization to another. In some firms which make to order, highly detailed estimates are prepared for every serious customer enquiry and voluminous records of previous quotations retained on file. If contract costing is required they may subsequently have to monitor progress, and then calculate and issue invoices for stage payments. On the other hand, those companies who make for stock may operate a telephone sales system and require immediate on-line access to data on available finished goods inventory and the ability to raise the necessary picking and despatch documentation at once.

In order to determine whether or not the sales function is operating satisfactorily, and to give an indication as to the company's computer requirements, some of the key aspects which should be considered are:

- How much duplication is there? For example, sales order written out by sales person, with prices and discounts, subsequently passed to a sales office where details are checked against records and a multi-copy sales order raised.

- How long does it take from the receipt of sales order details until it becomes a formal sales order recorded in the system? This time may be critical in terms of customer satisfaction and stock turnover.

- How many people are involved in the administration of a sales order from its receipt through recording, processing, raising an invoice and recording in the accounts receivable?

- How easy is it to check previous sales orders in terms of customer, product type, price, etc?

- If finished goods are not in stock, can the customer be given a quick and reasonably accurate estimate of when they can be shipped?

- Is there some means of reserving goods (either in stock or in production) against a specific sales order?

- Is the system responsive enough to produce a formal delivery note for a rush order?

- Would it be possible to ship goods to a customer that were subsequently not included on the invoice?

- What are the facilities for sales analysis and do they accord with the needs of the sales and marketing functions?

- What sales forecasts, if any, does the Sales Department give to production, and how detailed and accurate are they? Ask the production people and not just sales.

- How good is the system for informing the Sales Department on a daily/weekly basis about sales orders received? One company photocopied every one of the dozens of sales orders received and sent the relevant ones to each of its salesmen around the country every day.

- How many sales people have the authority, or take it upon themselves, to make promises to a customer which commit production resources, without consulting the production manager or controller?

- What is the attitude of other departments to the Sales Department: the way they operate, the quality of information they provide and their level of expectation?

- How easy is it to assess the order book and what level of detail is provided?

Design and process planning

Although these are normally two quite separate functions within a manufacturing organization, and not directly within the scope of a CAPM system under our definition, the way in which they are administered, indeed whether they are present or absent, is of major importance to some other functions in the manufacturing system. Whether or not the Design Department uses CAD techniques, and this may be an important consideration, it does provide data which is used in bills of material (BOM), itself a vital part of most CAPM systems. The main questions to be asked regarding the material and component data provided by the Design Department are:

- Is there any? Some design departments merely hand over the drawing to process planning or production, who are expected to identify everything and draw up a BOM.
- Is the data simply a list of materials, or is it in the form of a product structure, suitable for direct incorporation into a BOM?
- Is there a comprehensive and logical part-numbering/coding system in use, with the Design Department as the sole issuing authority?

The last question deals with one of the most frequently encountered problems and contentious issues encountered in investigations of this kind. In some instances the Design Department is the sole issuing authority. In other cases, either there is more than one system in operation, leading to confusion and duplication, or someone has invented a coding system so complex and all-embracing that even he or she doesn't fully understand it. On occasion, and not so infrequently, one discovers manufacturing organizations who do not have any kind of numeric or alpha-numeric parts and material identification whatsoever and who rely solely on description.

The selection and implementation of a materials classification or coding system is a subject of some importance and should be carried out with care. The essential points to bear in mind are:

- The system of numbering should be such as will allow future expansion in both numbers of materials and of product ranges.
- It should be simple to code any new material.
- The number of figures/letters should be kept as short as possible (see below).
- The figures/letters need not necessarily be 'significant', ie the ability to work out from any code the exact type, model, function, etc of the material. Many companies feel that they must have such a facility and expend much effort in devising one. This often gives rise to unwieldy coding numbers, 15 or 20 digits long, and the fact that each material can be described from its number often has no practical application being merely pseudo-scientific. One company which manufactured cars, trucks, earth-moving vehicles,

marine and aircraft engines used a universal 6-digit, non-significant coding system.

In those companies which have a process planning facility, it may take one of a number of forms. Where detailed estimates for customer quotation purposes are made in every case, this is in effect the rough equivalent of a process plan and this data can subsequently be used as the basis for production planning by the Process Planning Department. The planners in other manufacturing companies have no such data to assist them and must start afresh each time a new product or configuration is required. Just as with the Design Department, it is important that the investigator conducting the project should understand how process planning is carried out in the organization under review, because its form and make-up can have a major impact on the subsequent material and production control activities, the manufacturing efficiency of the organization and therefore on the selection of integrated CAPM systems.

Stores

Although the stores are properly a sub-section of the inventory control system (material control is seen as being comprised of the sub-sections purchasing, inventory control and production control), they will be treated separately for investigative purposes because they are the physical manifestation of an organization's inventory policies and procedures (or lack of them) and as such can be very revealing to the investigator. The effectiveness of a stores operation can be one of the major determinants in the success or failure of a manufacturing operation and too many companies see the stores as merely a collection of shelves and bins in which materials and components are stored until required on the shopfloor, where the real work begins, instead of recognizing it as an integral part of the manufacturing process. How often are the stores allocated some corner, an afterthought when the optimum shopfloor layout for manufacturing has been decided? How often are the stores partly manned by operatives who didn't quite make it on the shopfloor but are deemed to be adequate for the lesser task of handing out materials? From the widespread use of CAPM systems, with their emphasis on, and facilities for, material control, and from the recent interest in the JIT philosophy, manufacturers are fortunately more aware than ever of the need to control expensive materials and to spend more in achieving better control. It is a sound investment.

The function of any stores in a manufacturing environment is the supply of materials to the production operations (and for spares if required) in a timely and cost-effective manner. The detailed stores requirements will of course vary, dependent on the nature of manufacturing being carried out and the facilities which have to be provided, either to one site or several. Nevertheless, there are key features and functions which are common to all storage facilities in manufacturing operations, and it is important that these are borne in mind in any investigation into the effectiveness of this function and the ensuing evaluation of CAPM systems. Here are some of the main questions which should be answered when determining the effectiveness of a stores system and operation:

- How effectively is the recording of inventory movements carried out, eg raising of Goods Received Notes, communication of data to the inventory control system, issuing of materials against documentation such as material requisitions and kit lists?
- What access to the inventory control system, if any, do stores personnel have?
- How accurate is the physical inventory when compared with the 'book' stock?
- What location system is used, is it appropriate to the type of materials and methods used in the manufacturing operation and does it assist the stores operation rather than hinder it?
- Is the stores lockfast, with entry restricted to stores personnel, or is there free access to anyone who cares to walk in and help himself or herself?

The twin aspects of stores operation which are vital to good material control and therefore timely and efficient production, are speed and accuracy of information. When an inventory or production controller looks at inventory data, whether on a card or computer screen, that person must be confident that the data is correct, otherwise vital decisions about production schedules and the commitment of resources may be based on false premises. Nobody knows sooner than those who work with a system that it is not doing the required job quickly or effectively enough, and it is circumstances such as these in which 'unofficial' systems arise.

The physical appearance of any stores normally give a good indication as to the effectiveness of the inventory control system in use, whether manual or computerized. Poor housekeeping, unidentified materials or an inadequate location system can detract from even the best materials administration, and indeed adequate control can hardly be exercised in such an environment. This is especially so in the case of materials with special requirements, for example those with a specified shelf life in the food industry or with traceability requirements for use in civil or military aircraft. Stores procedures such as perpetual inventory must also be carried out with regularity and precision if they are to be effective in providing accurate data to the inventory records and assist in maintaining a balanced inventory. These aspects and others give pointers as to the suitability of the present systems and point the way towards any inventory control software which might be chosen.

Inventory control

The function of any inventory control system in a manufacturing company is similar to, but an extension of, that which has been given for stores. It is the control of materials in a cost-effective manner such that they supply production and spares requirements from a minimum inventory. A prerequisite of this is an appropriate inventory policy, something conspicuously lacking in many companies, or if present, given only passing acknowledgement. In investigating an inventory control system to determine its effectiveness and establish the requirements for possible computerization or the upgrading of a computer-based system, it must be remembered that it is not an end in itself but a service to manufacturing. The range and levels of stock to be maintained, its availability and quality, are all dictated by the scheduled production. Unfortunately this is an area, basic though it is, which has long been neglected by some companies either through misunderstanding of its importance or through the unwise luxury of lax management at the expense of high inventory. As has been demonstrated by the spread of CAPM systems into all sectors of manufacturing industry, the potential savings in some organizations are enormous.

Inventory control systems can range from the complex and detailed requirements of the aviation industry to the more simple needs of companies in the food industry which often have to purchase, in one lot at harvest time, their whole year's projected requirements for a particular commodity. Nevertheless, there are some common aspects to almost all inventory control systems and the following gives an indication of which areas might be examined:

- What are the organization's inventory policies regarding levels of inventory to be held (expressed monetarily), availability of materials for production and classification of obsolete inventory? Are these policies known and adhered to by the administrators of the inventory control system?
- How accurate are the inventory records compared to the physical inventory? Is the inventory controller aware of the accuracy level?
- How many weeks/months worth of inventory are held, both in raw materials and finished goods, and are there any rules by which this is regulated?
- If required, does the system supply quick and accurate information on finished goods inventory to the Sales Department and on raw materials to the production controller and the Manufacturing Department?

- What is the average percentage of materials shortage on the first pick of a kitting list? Alternatively, what percentage of work-in-process is waiting for materials?
- What is the value of sales lost due to raw material and/or finished goods stock-outs?
- Does the present system provide adequate analysis of raw materials and finished goods, in terms of usage frequency and obsolescence?

Purchasing

Being so closely allied to inventory control, indeed driven by it, the purchasing function cannot stand alone and should not be expected to do so. This section is not concerned with the commercial aspects of purchasing but with its operational aspects and the way in which the efficiency of a system can be assessed, although any increase in efficiency achieved might well give scope for improvements to the commercial aspect. This might be achieved by allowing the buyer to become more aware of other vendors; to negotiate better contracts from a position of strength because they can place blanket orders rather than buy one-off batches at a premium price to fulfil shortages; or evaluate alternative materials and components which may be more economical to use.

Purchasing departments within different organizations can range widely regarding the type and frequency of functions they are called upon to perform. For example, the purchasing of raw materials for a textile manufacturing plant which has machines dedicated to long production runs of fabric, will need a relatively straightforward system as most of its purchasing will be in bulk quantities for scheduled delivery. In a process industry there may only be one type of raw material bought, although various consumables might also be required. The needs of the average engineering jobbing shop might be considerably more complex, with a wide array of materials, components, sub-assemblies and sub-contract services being required, often in very small quantities and at short notice. The functions demanded of their purchasing systems would therefore be different and would determine the criteria against which present systems are to be evaluated.

It is nevertheless possible to formulate some basic criteria to be used in determining whether or not a purchasing system is performing according to requirements, such as:

- Are the materials and services demanded by inventory control provided in the specified timing, quality and quantity?
- Does the system keep track of all purchase orders placed for services and materials, showing the status of each one?

- Is there any form of vendor analysis available, to allow evaluation of performance and ranking of vendors?
- Is there adequate flexibility in the system so that the purchasing function can quickly respond to changes in production and spares demand?
- Does the system allow easy calculation of the financial commitment incurred by the placing of purchase orders?
- What vendor data is available in terms of materials and services supplied, prices, availability and alternatives?

Production planning

Just as in the previous section on purchasing we drew a distinction between what may be the relatively simple requirements of a flow process plant and the more sophisticated needs of a jobbing shop, so it is with the production control function. Where goods are produced continuously or in very large batches, the amount of detailed planning through the production process tends to be small, although this will of course depend on the complexity of the product being manufactured and the number of operations to be performed. In a fast-moving production environment, where the customer needs made-to-order products and expects short lead times, a more versatile system is required and more resources must be given over to the planning of production.

In looking at the methods used in an existing production planning system, as in any other system, one must bear in mind the single criterion which encompasses all others; that is 'fitness for purpose'. Has the purpose for which the systems are in operation been clearly defined and are the production needs being fulfilled? Three separate aspects of production planning need to be considered, the first being the planning of capacity in global terms. This would stem from some kind of master production schedule composed of firm and estimated sales orders, and would give a means of comparing projected load on production facilities with available capacity. The second is a means of determining capacity requirements in a much more detailed way, using product routing and queuing information to give a detailed analysis or simulation by work centre or by machine within work centre. Having established what capacity is available, the third aspect of consideration is some means of programming work through each stage of production. This is often referred to as shop scheduling and is primarily concerned with the sequencing of production activities.

Whatever they are called and in whatever way they manifest themselves, all three of these elements must be present in some form or other, even in a manual system, if a manufacturing facility is to have a reasonable chance of operating efficiency. Any investigation into the operational efficiency of a production planning system is largely comprised of determining to what extent these elements are present, how they are used and to what effect. The following are some key questions which should be asked of any production planning system:

- Is there a production plan drawn up and agreed to by all key departments ie sales, production, inventory and finance?
- How effective is the production planning system? There are various indicators when it is not performing as it should, such as regular failure to meet delivery dates, high work-in-process stocks, batches of work awaiting machine capacity, labour or materials, and idle labour because work is being held up at bottleneck operations.
- What is the extent and accuracy of data accessible for carrying out production planning? This might include a business plan or master production schedule, sales demand, machine and labour capacity at each work centre, and availability of materials. Does the lack of such information restrict the ability to plan production with the accuracy required?
- Does the Sales Department appreciate the constraints of time, capacity and lack of flexibility within which the production department must always work or do they, out of ignorance, make frequent, unrealistic delivery promises to customers?
- Are Production and Planning Departments aware of the sales-people's need for flexibility in manufacturing so that the organization can win sales by responding quickly to changing customer demands? Is data on current and planned production readily available to the Sales Department so that it can at all times operate within a realistic environment?
- How closely do the production and inventory control sections work? Do they see themselves as part of the same function?
- Is the present production control system, for example a wall-mounted planning board, used to its full extent or is it disused while the production controller carries out the planning in an informal manner using his 'experience'?

Production planning and control is the central administrative activity of any manufacturing system. Whether it is carried out well or not can make the difference between success and failure of the enterprise. If a company has poor production planning and control systems it may suffer from long and expensive queue times, high downtime and costly 'rush' jobs, all resulting in higher unit costs, long lead times and eventual loss of sales. When systems for the planning and control of production are appropriate for the needs of the business and well-administered, it is possible to achieve minimal work-in-process, short production lead times and low unit costs. These are the kind of targets which any investigation into production planning must consider. It is whether or not they are achieved that will determine the need for, and extent of, any changes to the system.

Shopfloor control

The actual process of manufacture is the most important of all activities within the organization and often the most difficult to control from a systems point of view. This is where so many of the other activities come together: inventory control, purchasing, production planning. At the same time, the processes which have to be controlled can be many and physically widespread in various work centres in different departments and perhaps even on separate sites. With all good intentions and the most diligent planning, this is often the point at which the system breaks down, where work-in-process clogs the arteries of production while idle time is being recorded at work centres, and 'firefighting' and overtime working at premium labour rates are the order of the day.

Much of this is the responsibility of shopfloor management and supervision but this can only be exercised on the basis of a sound work-in-process system, properly administered. Perhaps more so than any other part of manufacturing, many current shopfloor control systems rely heavily on documentation such as the following:
– Works orders
– Job cards
– Route cards
– Work-to lists
– Operations cards
– Material requisitions
– Kitting lists
– Drawings
– Quality assurance documentation
– Shortage lists

The purpose of these is, variously, to instruct, to identify, to record and thereby to control. An investigation into the workings of a current system must give consideration to these requirements and judge how well they are fulfilled. As previously mentioned, it is not advocated that documentation flowcharts are drawn up for all manufacturing systems but in this instance it may be helpful in understanding their sources, routes and purpose if there are a number of different documentation types in use. As systems develop over the years, often via what appears to be their own volition, it is easy for the number of documents to increase and still be maintained. Once in existence, and even if their original purpose no longer obtains, it is often difficult to do away with them. In examining systems and how they work, the investigator must take the view that the need for a piece of documentation must be proven in each case. This is especially so when CAPM systems are to be considered, with their vastly superior ability in electronic rather than documentary communication and control, since the specification of features and functionality should not come about simply because those attributes are currently present.

Some of the key questions which should be asked of any shopfloor control system in order to determine how well it meets the requirements are:

- What is the ratio between a) the net production time (the sum of all operation/process times for a standard-sized batch plus inter-operation transit time), and b) the total elapsed time between starting the first operation/process and completion of the last? Subtracting a) from b) gives the total non-productive time which does not add value to the product (ie set-up time, waiting for materials or labour, machine breakdown), and which is largely an avoidable cost of production. This can vary from close to zero in a JIT system, to almost indefinite length. On investigation, one company was found to have a batch production time of 4 hours [a)], and a batch throughput time of 16 weeks [b)].
- To what extent are shopfloor activities controlled by the 'official' system and to what extent by the 'unofficial' one?
- What detail if any is recorded on waiting time for materials, breakdowns, setters, tooling, etc? How easily can the progress of each job be tracked through the production operations and its status determined? Are productive hours recorded against specific jobs and is this data subsequently analysed?
- To what extent is the scheduling of jobs through work centres determined by the system and to what extent is it left to the judgement of shopfloor supervision?
- At the end of each week, how different is the actual production carried out from the planned production, and why?

Costing

The costing system with which we are concerned here is the gathering of actual costs of manufacture, for example by production batch, by model/type, or by works order/contract. For those organizations which make goods for stock in a flow process or in large batches, it may be sufficient that the average actual cost is calculated or that periodic sampling is done to ensure that costs remain within acceptable limits. Where small batches of disparate items are manufactured or unique products are produced to customer order, the precise actual cost of each job would need to be ascertained, otherwise there is no way of knowing what costs have been incurred or profit margin (or loss) has been achieved. Given that the whole object of any commercial enterprise is to make a profit, and that any charge against that profit should be of major concern, it is surprising how many companies do not know, and have no means of knowing with any exactitude, what any of their products cost to manufacture. Such a method (or non-method) of financial control might be termed 'bottom-line accounting', whereby in effect the company, at the end of each financial period, adds up all its revenue on the one hand and all its expenditure on the other. If the former is greater than the latter the company has made a profit. If not, it has broken even or made a loss.

Of course, many manufacturing managers will say that they know what their costs are in general terms and they have no need to expend time and effort in collecting every little detail against each product or process. Other companies, when asked how they have arrived at the selling price of a product will say that it's pitched at 3 per cent below the price of a rival product, and that as long as they are making a reasonable profit overall, that's good enough. The problem is that management have no way of knowing which products are being manufactured at a loss. Even in a profitable state, it is simply good management to know the costs incurred by each operation or process and by department, and to be able to monitor scrap costs, the utilization of labour and the level of overheads application in different manufacturing areas.

In evaluating a current system of cost collection, some of the main questions which should be asked are:

- What costs if any are collected during the manufacturing process and to what level of detail?
- How are labour hours recorded, including waiting time?
- Is the same overhead rate used for all manufacturing departments regardless of the different conditions within them, because there is no means of knowing and applying an appropriate rate for each department?
- Is there proper application of different labour rates to all of the production operations?
- Does the system allow for the recording of all actual costs and to what extent is this facility used, or is each actual cost taken as being the same as its estimated or standard cost because the gathering of actual costs is thought too difficult and time-consuming?
- Is there a means of readily comparing actual costs with planned costs at the level of detail required by the nature of the business?
- Is there a special costing requirement, such as contract costing, and how well is this fulfilled under the present system?

- What is the attitude of management and workforce to costs such as scrap, re-work, lost time?

Management information

As well as investigating the operational efficiency of manufacturing systems in each of the required areas, it is necessary also to find out how well they perform in analysing and presenting to management the mass of data which is constantly being gathered in a meaningful, concise and timely manner. Without this, and it is surprising how many systems fail to provide it fully, management cannot be expected to make informed decisions and run the enterprise efficiently. If the various levels of management are not receiving the data which they require or it is voluminous or late then this must be clearly identified and recorded. There can be a number of reasons for this, such as:

- management have never specified their information needs
- the systems have not been designed to gather the data required
- the data which is collected cannot be analysed in the required format
- the methods of data collection and analysis are so cumbersome and slow that the information is merely the record of an historical event and almost useless by the time it is received.

All possibilities should be thoroughly investigated and evaluated against the model of an efficient system. The requirements of a system for manufacturing management information centre on each area of activity and will vary according to the type of manufacturing methods employed and for the different levels of management within the organization. For example:

Sales: quantity, type, market sector, lost sales

Materials: stock value, usage, critical shortages, obsolescence

Costing: planned/actual cost of each product, labour costs, material costs, overhead costs, cost performance by plant, department, work centre and machine

Production: production program, performance by product, work centre and department, work-in-process levels.

Attitudes to present company systems

During a feasibility study, when investigating the reasons for strengths or weaknesses in present methods of working, it is important to distinguish between the systems in theory, their everyday usage and the attitude of those who use them. Even a good system can be inefficient in operation because the users take an antipathetic attitude towards it, usually because of inadequate training for its use or the belief that it is the wrong system for their needs. Discussions should be held with all key users of the system in each of the areas which are being evaluated, so that their views and opinions are given and not simply a description of how the system does (or should) work.

And what is the attitude of middle and top management to the present manufacturing systems within their organization? Do they know very much about them – or care, except insofar as they broadly meet with requirements and literally "produce the goods"? Do not be surprised if, having had the present methods and their shortcomings described, senior management disputes the findings with the investigator. The system that the manager has in mind is probably theoretical and if it ever was in operation, has long since ceased to be so. Unless shown why it should be otherwise, people who operate a system regularly will eventually take the line of least resistance and adapt the 'official' system to their own 'unofficial' one (which of course can be an improvement).

CHAPTER 5

Assessing the Feasibility

Consultation with personnel

In the last chapter we described the process of gathering information and showed some of the areas in which this might take place. The general objective of this is to provide sufficient data to enable an evaluation of the strengths and weaknesses of the present systems and to allow a judgement to be made as to the likely benefits of implementing a CAPM system. This is an essential part of the selection and implementation process. Not only does it help to define present shortcomings and future needs, it also gives people a formal opportunity to voice their opinion, possibly for the first time, about the systems with which they have to work. In other words, not only must management be looking for the best solutions to problems, they must be seen to be looking for them diligently, and in the process, tapping the huge reserves of knowledge and experience held by their own personnel.

There is no point in going too far the other way – approaching individuals in various departments, telling them that new systems are being considered and simply asking them what kind of features they would like in the systems. You are liable to get the answer "What have you got?" It is not the object of this part of the exercise simply to go around collecting 'wish lists' from each section in the organization. If only it was as easy as that. And yet this is the way in which some companies operate, submitting the list of desired features in each area such as purchasing, inventory control and work-in-process to a software vendor in the fond hope that the resultant suite of manufacturing programs will exactly fit the organization's requirements. Never mind that the only features specified (and probably incompletely) were those that came to mind at the time or that the persons making the selection did not know about the various options which were available in CAPM systems.

It is generally true that once an 'appropriate' package system has been selected, the vendor will go through each program in detail with your personnel to determine the exact configuration of each program *within its limitations*. It can be at this time that the realization dawns that the system does not cater for some of the organization's key requirements, or at the very least has some niggling shortcomings which might easily have been avoided had more knowledge been applied at an earlier stage. If this happens there are three options: a) throw out the software (and possibly also the hardware) and start again – a very expensive solution; b) where possible, have the systems tailored to the company's specific requirements – this may be expensive but at the very least takes time and effort; c) accept the system as it is and tell everyone it's perfect for the job, until it has been around long enough to justify throwing it out and starting again – possibly the worst solution of all as it is not only a bad capital investment but may prejudice personnel against computer systems in general and will certainly not improve their opinion of management ability. The only answer, in the words of the quality assurance people, is to get it right first time. You can't afford any other way.

The feasibility report

At this stage in the project, and it may be the final stage if it is shown that computerization is going to offer few cost-effective benefits, a report will need to be written by the investigator, giving details of findings, making comparisons and drawing conclusions from the available information. The report may only be an interim one for the steering committee to consider, or it may be drawn up by them for the consideration of the board of directors prior to the next stage of the project. Like all reports, it should be informative and concise. It should not merely be a brief summary of findings and recommendations but should be expansive enough to lay out the relevant facts in some detail and draw conclusions from them. That is to say, it must set out to convince the reader of the correctness of its conclusions. Whether or not the project goes ahead should depend on it. Even in a small organization there can be two or more 'camps', and it is helpful if the report writer knows this before putting pen to paper so that he or she can better answer their objections. These factions can support widely differing courses of action. For example:

- Those who oppose computerization of any sort on a matter of principle and say that it's an unnecessary expense.
- Those who say that the present systems are perfectly adequate and that they are just not run properly. This is often a valid argument. It is all too easy for the shortcomings of working methods or poor attitude to be blamed on the system, especially by those who exhibit the shortcomings.

- Those who want to computerize everything possible, on the grounds that anything computerized must be better than a manual version.
- Those who say that it would be nice if such systems did work but life isn't that easy; that this kind of thing was tried before and didn't work; or that the company down the road have just thrown out their CAPM system because of non-performance.

If the report is to recommend that inadequate benefits would come from computerization then this should be clearly stated, accompanied by the relevant arguments. Where the evidence shows that implementing a CAPM system would be cost-effective for the organization, the report should not only present the facts and recommendations but attempt to steer a sensible middle course between the views of the extremist camps and answer their objections.

Whatever form the report takes, it should at least contain the following elements:
- a description of the present systems
- strengths and weaknesses in the systems
- general shortcomings
- recommendations
- a financial assessment.

Other aspects of the study and information coming from it can also be included, but only insofar as they are germane to the case which is being made. Some explanation and expansion upon these subject headings may be helpful.

Description of the systems
A general description of the present systems should be given, showing their main functions and relationships with each other. This can include a systems flowchart but this should only be in the form of an outline. There is no point in spending time drawing detailed flowcharts which include every piece of documentation in the organization, in order to prove how inefficient (or efficient) the systems are. This should be done for each sub-system in a few succinct sentences, and if it cannot be done then there may not be a strong argument for change or it may have been poorly presented. It has to be remembered that many of the report readers will be non-technical people who might be reluctant to devote time to understanding a complex flowchart or will be prejudiced against the report and its conclusions by a mass of technical detail. If the report seeks to explain and persuade, it must do so in the readers' language.

Strengths and weaknesses
Details of the strengths and weaknesses in each part of the current system should be given, how these assist or detract from the efficient running of each function and some indication as to the effect they

have on the profitability of the business. This is a crucial section of the report and the one which will largely determine whether or not CAPM is feasible for the company. The financial aspects of this section should not be neglected as they are the means of expressing the consequences of the systems' shortcomings.

General shortcomings
Some indication should be given of any other shortcomings which emerge during the course of the investigation and which may have a bearing on subsequent computerization, such as poor systems discipline, lack of experience or staff training (there is no need to personalize it at this stage), or ignorance of the basic principles upon which systems such as inventory or production control are based. It is not sufficient to identify and describe those functions which do not operate effectively. The shortcomings of personnel must be separated from those of the system before a fair evaluation of the system can be made.

General recommendations
Broad recommendations as to the course of action to be taken should be made in the knowledge that more detailed information will be available at a later stage, such as the actual cost of software and hardware. Nevertheless, a clear evaluation of the present systems should be presented and comparisons made with the likely benefits from implementation of a new CAPM system. As well as giving a suggested plan of action, the report should give an indication as to how long the implementation period will be and the likely implications for other key parts of the business, such as design, marketing and distribution.

Financial assessment
This should be an assessment of the financial implications of any proposed action *and of inaction*. The cost of doing nothing should always be given where possible, it being the loss of those estimated savings to be had from computerization whether in the form of continuing inventory losses, over-investment in work-in-process or loss of sales through customer dissatisfaction. This financial assessment should not be a full-scale, cost-benefit anaysis – that will come later. What is required is a few figures giving orders of magnitude for expenditure and revenue. For example:

a) *New CAPM systems:*
Expenditure

hardware:	100,000
software:	80,000
training and implementation:	50,000
	230,000

Savings   reduction in raw materials inventory: 60,000
                                reduction in work-in-process: 45,000
                                    profit on increased sales: 20,000
                                            labour savings: 15,000
                                    lower scrap and re-work: 10,000
                    reduction in finished goods inventory: 80,000
                                                        *   230,000

* These would be realized in the first full year after all systems became operational.

b) *Present systems:*
Continuing losses, per annum   230,000

This of course is far from being a proper cost/benefit analysis and takes no account of such things as cash flows and payback periods, but it is only intended to show in summary whether or not there is a *prima facie* case for proceeding with the CAPM project. The decision as to the feasibility of computerization may not rest solely on whether it is financially justifiable at the site where it would be implemented. There may for instance be a requirement for systems integration with another site within the organization. Alternatively, there may be a request from customers for an interface between your computerized sales order processing system and their purchase ordering system for direct transfer of data. Another consideration in the computerization decision-making process may be that of being seen by vendors, customers and competitors to be taking advantage of the latest technological developments, although since the benefits from this would be difficult to quantify, its influence on the final decision is likely to be marginal.

Whether or not the investigation and report is being carried out by an external consultant or by someone from within the organization, a presentation of the investigation findings, conclusions and recommendations should be given to those who will make the final decision on computerization. Such decisions should not go through 'on the nod', although this is not uncommon even when large and expensive projects are being considered. While it is easier for those advocating computerization that a project is approved in this way, it should be avoided if possible. Those persons making the decision should know the reasons for change being required. Without a well-argued case in the report this will not be so and there will be no record of justification if the project subsequently goes awry or does not deliver the promised benefits. Besides, it is merely good management to conduct the whole of the project in a professional manner.

The presentation need not be sophisticated. Its object is to show clearly and concisely the main findings, the efficiency or otherwise of the present systems, and the benefits, if any, that will accrue from implementing a new CAPM system. If the organization has slow and inefficient manual systems, then it should not be too difficult to win the argument for computerization, provided that the capital can be made available or the directors are willing to enter into a leasing agreement for the hardware and software. At the other extreme, if a full or part CAPM system has been in use for some time, it may be extremely difficult to persuade those familiar with it to have it replaced, with all the disruption, learning and cost which this involves.

It is preferable if the presentation is given and the report distributed immediately afterwards. This does not give the opportunity for questions arising from the report to be raised there and then, although a good presentation and question session should cover this. What this method does give is impact on those in attendance, and this may make the difference between acceptance and rejection of the case for computerization. If the report is a lengthy one, because the complexity of the systems demands it, those who consider it may not have either the time nor the inclination to read the whole thing from cover to cover. They will simply skim through the text, examine the figures in some detail and take their lead from the summary which should be given at the front of the report. Many of the facts unearthed may go unread and the carefully constructed arguments will be lost. A presentation of the findings and recommendations in the report, where one has the undivided attention of the decision-makers, is an opportunity not to be missed.

The computer strategy

After the decision has been taken to proceed to the following stage in the computerization project, in the ensuing enthusiasm it is all too easy to rush ahead and begin to look at possible CAPM systems in an unstructured and haphazard way. Instead, time should be taken to draw up a computer strategy which will encompass all of those systems elements likely to be acquired in the near future and others which might be of use in the medium to long term. Every system which might possibly be needed should be considered. It is better to have allowed for the possibility of having a contract costing system for example, than to discount it at the beginning only to find that two or three years hence the company could benefit from one but cannot have it as part of the system implemented. It is for this reason among others that the question of systems computerization should be considered in the light of the company's five-year business plan, in which indications of new markets and products will point the way to future systems requirements.

So, what is a computer strategy? There are no hard and fast rules, but it can be seen as a long-term plan which sets out an organization's computer-oriented goals, the methods by which these are to be achieved, their sequence and timing. Naturally, it is derived from the organization's business goals, as it is an expression of some of the resources needed to achieve those goals. It should be broad in scope and at the same time give reasonable detail, and while it could be drawn up by the project leader and the steering committee, it would need the imprimatur of the board of directors to ensure that it does accord with business goals and that the level of ongoing expenditure is acceptable. The computer strategy should be seen as the core document from which the project leader, steering committee and implementers take their lead, as well as a permanent record of corporate computing goals. It need amount to no more than one or two pages, and a proposed computer strategy often forms part of the report on findings and recommendations discussed above. Even if it does not, some kind of strategy should be formulated, and guidelines for this are given below.

Background

This should merely serve to set the scene by giving background information from relevant parts of the organization's business plan, an outline of the systems currently in use and any other matters which directly affect the choice or execution of the strategy, such as group hardware policy (eg must all be IBM-compatible), or the need for interface with other external systems. It should give the rationale which underlies the strategy and the premises on which it is based. It is important that this is made clear, given re-evaluation may be necessary if circumstances change sufficiently.

Objective

This should be a simple statement of the goal at which the strategy is aimed, an encapsulation of the policy and the achievement described in terms of the terminal state. An example of this could be:

"To have a complete CAPM system fully operational in all sales, manufacturing and financial functions, capable of interfacing with pre-production systems, as a major instrument in the achieval of our corporate policy of Total Quality Management."

Functions

This section lays out the strategy in some detail, commencing with a description of each function to be computerized, together with a brief explanation. The sequence and timing of the implementation should be given, as well as the type of software envisaged, such as bespoke written or package programs, and where necessary, an indication of hardware type or other considerations. For example:

Inventory control

In order to reduce the company's dependence on high raw materials and finished stocks, and at the same time to increase the service levels of finished goods to the customer, this will be the first CAPM system to be implemented. When operational it will give immediate benefits in terms of positive cashflow from inventory reductions, an improvement in finished goods availability highly visible to the customer, and the opportunity of increased sales as a result. It will also pave the way for the other materials control systems (BOM, MRP and purchasing) and give accurate data to both the Sales and Production Departments. As a pilot program, inventory control will be given a trial run in the Machines Division before being fully introduced both there and in the Liquids Division.

Materials requirements planning (MRP)

MRP will be implemented in the Machines Division (including provision for spares) as soon as its prerequisites are fully operational, ie inventory control, BOM, MPS. Through the use of MRP, the supply of raw materials, components and sub-assemblies to the Machines Division production line will be significantly improved, increasing operational efficiency, reducing downtime awaiting material and lowering manufacturing costs in line with the 5-year business plan. MRP is not an appropriate technique for the Liquids Division and will not be implemented there, so the planning of material requirements will continue to be carried out by the current method, but using the inventory control and purchasing programs in the new CAPM system.

Work-in-process control

Following the successful implementation of the production planning system for both the Machines and Liquids Divisions, the work-in-process program will be introduced simultaneously into both sites. There are three main objectives in implementing this program: a) to assist in the reduction of work-in-process, b) to give the ability to track works orders through production and c) to provide adequate data for customer enquiries on order progress.

Either in the body of the text or as a separate listing specific targets should be given for each function included in the strategy. These should invariably contain two elements, namely quantity and timing. It is essential that realistic targets are drawn up before the implementation process begins so that everyone concerned knows what is to be achieved and in what timescale. There is no point in these being vague or unquantified as they are intended to be used later as a means of measuring achievement. Figures should be given for each expected amount of increase or reduction in such things as stock levels, work-in-process, manufactured output, sub-contract work and so forth, together with the time by which they are to be achieved. Examples of such targets are given below.

Sales order processing
Reduction in time taken to process a sales order.
Increased 'hit rate' for first-time pick ex-stock.

Inventory control
Reduction in raw materials stockholding.
Reduction in finished goods stockholding.
Increase in raw material availability/ reduced production downtime due to raw materials shortage.
Increase in finished goods availability.

Production control
Reduced work-in-process.
Reduced production downtime due to shortage of work.
Increased productivity.

Purchase order processing
Reduced vendor lead times.
Increase in number of scheduled orders placed on vendors.
Reduction in unit cost of raw material.

Costing
Standard/planned cost and actual costs for each raw material, component, sub-assembly and finished product.

In addition to detail of this kind, there might be added some proposals for other computerized systems which would interface with, or have some bearing on, the main CAPM ones, such as CAD or shopfloor data collection with bar-code readers.

Implementation timetable

Some kind of general guidelines must be given for the period over which the CAPM systems are to be implemented as well as the timing of the various stages. These timings may well be required to synchronize with milestones in the business plan, such as the start-up of a new production line, a move into a different market sector or the commencement of new administrative systems. In any event, the timing should never simply be arbitrary. At a later time, when the actual system has been chosen and a detailed implementation plan is being drawn up, precise timing of each event will be necessary. It must also be borne in mind that some modules or programs from CAPM systems have to be implemented in a certain sequence, for example inventory control and bill of materials before materials requirements planning. At this juncture it is sufficient that a planned implementation period is given, say 14 months, and that of the main stages, thus:

	Machines Division	Liquids Division	Month
Stage 1 *Material Control*			
Inventory control	x	x	2
Bill of material	x	x	2
Master production scheduling	x	x	3
Material requirements planning	x		6
Purchase order processing	x	x	7
Stage 2 *Production Control*			
Works documents	x	x	4
Routings	x		7
Capacity planning	x	x	8
Shopfloor scheduling	x		10
Work-in-process	x		12
Costing	x		14
Stage 3 *Sales and Financial*			
Sales order processing	x	x	10
Sales analysis	x	x	10
Accounts receiveable	x	x	12
Accounts payable	x	x	13
General ledger	x	x	14

Resources

As part of the agreed computer strategy it is helpful if some indication is given of the amount of corporate, and where appropriate, departmental resources which are to be committed to the project. As with other aspects of the strategy, this should not be detailed at this stage. As the implementation of all but the most modest CAPM systems (eg a 'stand alone' capacity planning program) is expensive of resources, rules must be laid down at an early stage and certainly before anyone starts looking seriously at possible systems.

Around this time the question arises as to whether the systems required should determine the capital expenditure on hardware and software, or whether the amount of resources available should determine the system acquired. This is a difficult question. Good systems form one of the frameworks upon which many successful manufacturing companies are built and one would normally expect to implement the best available for the particular application. Yet harsh financial realities inevitably intervene and often it is a case of accepting the best system for the available money. A recent example of this was a small engineering company which manufactured components for the defence industry. The company wished to implement a CAPM system covering all functions from sales order processing, through material control to manufacturing, and would ideally have liked a system specifically designed for that industry, with special features such as contract costing and serial number traceability throughout. The business was simply not generating enough profit to justify purchasing such a system and the payback period would have been excessive. It had to settle for a less sophisticated suite of programs at half the price of a defence contractor system and continue to use some of its manual procedures where necessary. We will see how to specify the requirements and the wishes of each function within a manufacturing business, how to submit it to vendors and critically examine their responses. Whether or not an organization is willing to commit the necessary resources to acquire those systems must remain a matter for its executive officers.

CHAPTER 6

Specifying Requirements

Drawing up the CAPM systems specification containing the requirements of the organization is one of the most important tasks in the whole project. It is against this document that potential systems vendors will tender, and those tenders will be evaluated against the specification when they are received by your company. A systems specification, incorporated in the larger invitation to tender (ITT) has the function of communicating in clear and unequivocal terms what is required from the vendor by way of hardware and software performance. The specification which would need to be prepared for bespoke CAPM systems would be very different from that required for the package programs we wish to acquire. Every aspect of systems, to the smallest detail, would need to be written down, every parameter defined. It would be a time-consuming and expensive job, and for the majority of small to medium-sized manufacturing companies with normal requirements, one which has now been made unnecessary by the development of sophisticated software catering for all but the most exotic requirements. That is what you are paying for when you purchase a suite of CAPM package programs: a ready-made product available from stock which incorporates as standard all or most of the features your organization requires. Much of the spadework has been done, and this is reflected in the relative simplicity of the systems specification. Simplicity of form, that is, not necessarily of content.

The specification format

It must be said at the outset that there is no set format for this type of specification, so there is nothing to stop you from drawing one up in whatever way you choose. The method and layout described here and given in the sample specification in Appendix I is one which has become quite common and appears to be acceptable to vendors of computer systems. The main text consists of a list of the key features required in each area of manufacturing, broadly corresponding to the programs or modules found in many package CAPM systems today. Some companies adopt a narrative technique, as they feel that it better explains the expected relationship between different functions. The choice is yours. One advantage of the 'list' approach is that it allows the ranking of features according to their necessity or desirability and a subsequent accurate comparison of tenders with each other and with the original specification. This is not easy to do when the key features to be evaluated are embedded in blocks of descriptive text.

Although it involves a little more work, the ranking or weighting of the features required is well worthwhile, otherwise equal weight would be given to such disparate features as material traceability on the one hand and an alternative routing facility on the other, when in fact one feature was essential and the other merely desirable. As the required features are built up, they should be classified in one of three categories according to their importance, namely necessary, desirable and marginal (N, D and M), as described in Chapter Three. A points system can then be applied, for example where $N=5$, $D=3$ and $M=2$, so that the total number of actual points for each tender can be compared with the total number possible as per the CAPM system specification.

Hardware, software and maintenance

Before looking in detail at the systems specification we should briefly consider the other part of what makes up the ITT, the initial section which deals with general questions regarding hardware and software, maintenance and contractual terms. This section is every bit as important as the subsequent specification and on no account should it be omitted. There is little point in obtaining hardware and software which exactly meets with your company's requirements only to discover subsequently that the training costs are three times what you expected or that the hardware maintenance has been sub-contracted to an incompetent organization.

The first section of the ITT would normally consist of a short introduction followed by a company profile, giving a description of the company's products and methods of manufacture as well as the reasons for wishing to implement a CAPM system. An example of this can be seen in Appendix I. The section which follows this consists of various questions under a heading such as Tender Requirements and deals with hardware, software, maintenance and other key subjects. It is vital that the potential supplier answers all these questions (and others where relevant) so that you are in no doubt about any aspect of the goods and services he or she is offering. It is preferable too that the answers are given in the same format as the questions have been put, otherwise considerable time will be spent finding the information you want in the often sizeable tenders received. This section will be considered in some detail in Chapter Seven, Evaluation of Tenders.

Under the section entitled Proposed Computer Systems, a list of the required programs or modules should be given, followed by a few paragraphs about the CAPM system as a whole and any specific needs such as the provision of source code to allow subsequent modification of the software by the user organization. Let us now look at each manufacturing function in turn and consider some of the features that might be incorporated into the systems specification.

Sales order processing and invoicing

The functional requirements from a sales order processing (SOP) system can vary considerably, dependent upon the nature and frequency of sales orders received and the degree of sophistication with which they need to be handled. At one end of the spectrum there is the made-to-order capital goods manufacturer who carries out a comprehensive estimating process for most if not all the firm sales enquiries received. At the other extreme, for a company which manufactures products for stock, there may be a requirement for a SOP program which supports a telephone sales operation, with direct entry of customer requirements into the computer and the ability to give an immediate response as to stock position and expected delivery dates.

The main areas of functionality to be considered when deciding upon a SOP module are:

a) *Form and content of sales orders* – are the products sold ex-stock, with a simple description and part number held on file, or are they made-to-order and require an extensive description to be written each time? Is there a need to cater for scheduled/call-off orders? Is the order in the form of a contract, with 'milestones' and stage payments?
b) *Pricing* – are products to be priced from a list of standard prices or individually, dependent upon the actual cost of manufacture? What degree of sophistication is required for the discounting facility?
c) *Documentation* – which documentation will the SOP module be required to produce: order acknowledgement, picking list, advice notes, invoice, pro-forma invoice, etc.
d) *Sales analysis* – what level of sophistication is required in the analysis of sales orders: sales and profit by value and percentage; by sales area, by salesman, by customer, etc?

e) *Interfaces* – with which other modules does SOP need to interface: finished goods inventory control for automatic downdating of stock levels; sales ledger for checking credit status and to which sales are posted; to the works order program, enabling works orders to be created from sales order data; to ancillary systems, such as CAE?

In addition to an SOP and invoicing module there may also be a requirement for a sales forecasting function. This may be part of SOP but is more likely to be a separate program. The main parameters for such a program are the extent and level of sophistication of the forecasting database, the forecasting techniques available such as weighted average, and whether or not it allows for trends and seasonality.

Product data management

This is a category which covers a number of key areas of data creation, storage and retrieval, including bills of material, production routeings and information on work centres. It is from these databases among others, that modules such as Materials Requirements Planning (MRP) and capacity planning draw data which is then used to calculate and determine output. The functionality required may be simple, where very few raw materials are used and there is little assembly work, and where only a few work centres are involved in the manufacturing process. An example of this would be the type of components produced by a foundry. At the other extreme is the building of aircraft, where the manufacturing routes are many and various and the bill of material large and complex. The systems requirements of these two types of manufacture are quite different and it is the Product Data Management modules which most clearly reflect this. While a system which would support aircraft manufacture would certainly do all that was required of it in a foundry, it would be a gross over-specification and not cost-effective. The system which was merely adequate for foundry work would of course be of little use in aircraft construction. It is important that the requirements of the Product Data Management modules are clearly understood, initially by the future users and subsequently by the potential vendors. Here are some of the main points to bear in mind when this section is being considered:

a) *Bill of material (BOM)* – this file holds, in hierarchical form, details of all materials and components required to manufacture a given item. How many levels will be required? Do bills need to hold actual and standard costs for each raw material, component and sub-assembly? Is there need for alternatives to be held for each part on a bill? Will you need to create similar bills of material from those already on file?

b) *Routings* – for each product to be manufactured, this file holds

69

details of each operation to be carried out and its sequence. Do you need to discriminate between made-in and bought-out parts? Will the ability be required to define which operators and machines are available and their respective limitations? Would the ability to give a preference rating for an operator on a machine type give greater routing efficiency? Do you wish to include inspection and/or sub-contract operations in routings? Will you require to record alternative routings?

c) *Work centres* – this file holds data on each work centre, through one or more of which each product or batch of products moves during the production process. Will it be necessary to classify some individual machines as work centres? Is a standard capacity required for each works centre? How do you wish labour and overhead rates to be handled? What kind of enquiries/reports are available from this module?

d) *Interfaces* – the primary interfaces required will be between these files and some of the following which are to be implemented: MRP, capacity planning and scheduling, inventory control.

Inventory control

Along with capacity planning and scheduling, this is one of the key sub-systems within any manufacturing operation, whether those systems are computerized or manual. The proper control of raw materials and finished goods stock is axiomatic in running an efficient production company, especially in these days of high rates of borrowing and fierce international competition for manufactured goods markets. It is vital that an inventory control program is selected which is in accord with your company's requirements, and the key to this lies in correct specification. Here are some of those features which should be considered.

a) *Item master file* – this file holds the static data on each raw material/component, such as part number, description, material, etc. Will material traceability, either in batch or serial number mode be required? What kind of stores/bin location system will be in operation after implementation of the new Inventory Control module (eg multi-store, multi-location)? How many different units of measure are used for raw materials, and is it required that they can be converted automatically from a purchased unit of measure (eg weight) to the one in which inventory is held (eg linear)? What size of part number field is required, and is there provision for a drawing number also?

b) *Inventory data* – this can broadly be described as the maintaining of data some of which is fairly static, such as procurement lead times, and some which is volatile, for example the in-stock and on-order levels of each raw material. In whatever way your inventory is currently managed, it must be remembered that the introduction of a MRP or JIT system for example, could radically change inventory control requirements, and therefore the functionality required of this module. The following are some of the main points to be considered. Will the system need to cater for re-ordering of materials by the order-point method, via MRP or both? What inventory valuation method will be used? How will stock be issued to production (eg in kits, in bulk)? Are goods received notes (GRNs) required and pre-acceptance inspection procedures in operation? Does your company operate release note procedures or require the maintenance of shelf-life records (eg for safety-critical materials/components)? What audit trail facilities are required?

c) *Documentation and reports* – which documentation is required from the module, and should it be bar-coded (eg picking and binning lists with inventory locations)? What reports are required and need to be specified, or is a report generator available as standard?

d) *Inventory maintenance* – will a system of cycle counting be in operation and if so, will the system be required to determine which items are to be counted and produce the necessary lists? Is it intended that ABC inventory analysis be used? Are stocktake sheets available with/without current inventory levels?

e) *Interfaces* – with which modules would Inventory Control need to interface; for example SOP, Purchase Order Processing, MRP, Costing, Financial?

Master production scheduling

By taking into account such factors as sales forecasts, sales orders, material and productive capacity availability, and testing them by rough-cut capacity planning, the master production schedule (MPS) program produces an anticipated production schedule, in terms of dates and quantities of end items. This data is the primary input for the MRP program.

There are a number of variations possible in the MPS programs. The main elements which should be considered are: the requirement for rough-cut capacity planning; how the program time-phases data, ie is it a bucketed or bucketless system? What is the content of the MPS report, eg forecast demand , customer orders, planned receipts and projected inventory for each product planned as a stock item? Does it handle made-to-order items and spares? Will the program be required to support net change or regenerative processing in MRP? What length of planning horizon will be needed in the MPS program?

Material requirements planning

The technique of computerized MRP can be applied to many types of manufacturing industry, although it is often seen as being primarily of use in production processes where there are a large number of assembly operations and many raw materials have to be managed, such as in the automotive industry. In those industries with relatively simple manufacturing processes and little or no assembly work, such as plastics moulding or glassmaking, the benefits to be gained from the application of MRP are limited. Nonetheless, the technique has been applied with success to many different industries. In addition, it is now also seen as a good foundation upon which to develop a JIT system.

An MRP module should not be installed simply because it is a technique in widespread use, and has for some years been put forward as the answer to many production management problems, just as JIT and OPT are now being similarly described. It is a simple materials planning technique, the essence of which can be explained in five minutes, and which has been in use for hundreds if not thousands of years in one form or another. Here are some of the criteria which you might use to decide whether or not it is right for your business and what features would be required in it.

Is your materials planning and control system a simple one, with relatively few materials, or is it complex and time-consuming, with many materials to be handled? Is there room for significant reduction in raw materials inventory and work-in-process? How rapidly does change in finished product and therefore raw material demand take place? If rapidly, this would suggest a regenerative system rather than a net change one. What length of planning horizon will be required and should the system operate in bucketed or bucketless mode? Which lot-sizing techniques will be used, eg fixed order quantity, lot for lot? Does the system need to have a pegging facility? Which interfaces will be required with other modules, such as MPS, finished goods and raw materials inventory control, purchase order processing and BOM?

Purchase order processing

This module is an integral part of any material control suite of programs (ie Inventory control, MRP). It offers the ability to maintain tight control on the placing and tracking of purchase orders on vendors and the assessment of vendor performance. Like MRP, it is especially useful when the material control system is complex, with a large number of materials to be procured, necessitating many purchase orders and vendors. In environments where this is not so, such as in some process industries, there may be little benefit to be gained from the implementation of a Purchase Order Processing module. Here are some of the main features which should be considered.

a) *Requisitions* – will automatic tracking of requisitions and the purchase orders generated from them be required? In what format (eg requisition reports, on-line enquiry displaying both requisitions and purchase orders)? Will MRP be required to generate requisitions? Does the system need to automatically group requisitions by item/vendor to reduce the number of purchase orders generated?

b) *Purchase orders* – will the system be required to handle non-inventory purchases? Will there be blanket orders, with multiple delivery dates/materials on one order, with separate tracking of each? Can over/under quantities be accepted as fulfillment of an order? What detail will be required on purchase order enquiries and reports (eg overdue reports, purchase variance report by volume and value)? Will the system be required to handle vendor quotations?

c) *Receipts* – how will the system update the inventory control files on raising of a purchase order and receipt of materials? Will it need to print GRN? What tracking detail will be required (eg vendor to dock, dock to inspection)? What screen enquiries need to be provided? Will rejected material need to be monitored? How will purchase orders and vendor Invoices be matched?

d) *Interfaces* – will interfaces be required with the Inventory Control, MRP, Accounts Payable modules?

Capacity planning and scheduling

The amount of sophistication required in a computerized planning and scheduling system will depend on the complexity of the production processes and the degree of control desired to exercise over them. Some companies prefer to take a broad approach to these functions, with capacity being planned in a general way and little scheduling of jobs on an individual basis. There are a number of reasons why this might be so:

- most jobs have short run times and therefore detailed planning and scheduling would be wasted effort
- the manufacturing process may be of unpredictable length and content
- there may be a need to have a greater flexibility in executing rush orders than a planning and scheduling system would ordinarily allow.

As with other functions, the nature of the business in question will determine what type of system will be most suitable. A case can often be made for the current administrative practices to be changed in order to fit in with a proposed new CAPM system, although too often companies are unwilling to countenance this. On the other hand, changes should never be made which might affect the essential nature of the business. If, for example, customers expect a 'while-you-wait' manufacturing or repair service, it's unlikely that they will accept its demise simply because a new planning and scheduling system has been implemented. The system must never be the master of the business but merely a servant to it.

Some of those featu.es which may be considered in capacity planning and scheduling are:

a) *Capacity planning* – will it be possible to differentiate between those loads created by released and planned works orders? Will the system need to carry out finite planning, infinite planning or both? How useful would a simulation or 'what-if' facility be to the production control department? Would a graphic display of work centre load profiles be required? Will there be a need for the load profile report to segregate the different types of works orders, ie planned orders, firm planned orders, released orders and simulated orders? How does the system handle the backlog of incomplete operations?

b) *Scheduling* – what are the criteria for calculating the work loading priority sequence and would it need to be over-ridden on computer? Would backward or forward scheduling be more appropriate to your production needs? How stable is the demand on the production facility, eg addition of unplanned and removal of planned operations from a works order? How much outwork and sub-contract operations will be handled? Are manufacturing operations ever performed out of sequence or overlapped?

Shopfloor control

This is an area of critical importance in any manufacturing operation, and one which is too often under-resourced in terms of control systems and data-gathering capability. It is here that due delivery dates can be met or missed, that profitable manufacture can be carried out and work-in-process kept to a minimum. The often complex business of launching works orders onto the shopfloor, monitoring progress through many different operations as well as making changes and recording performance is difficult to carry out efficiently. The level of control required of work-in-process will of course vary from one manufacturing plant to another, but there are three essential elements for any such system; it must be capable of raising the required documentation (some systems have a separate program for this eg works documentation); of providing details on the status of all released works orders; and of recording production performance (including costs, which is the subject of a separate section). Some of the main features which should be considered are given below.

Which documentation will need to be produced (eg material requisitions, job cards, operations cards, route cards)? How often will the progress of a works order be updated (eg after each operation or on the completion of all operations at the time of closing a works order)? Which reports, such as overdue operations and works orders, will be required? Will a system of bar-coded, shopfloor data collection be required? What level of tracking will be required for sub-contract operations? What degree of performance analysis will be necessary (eg by works order, operation, operator, standard versus actual)? What interfaces with other CAPM systems will be required (eg inventory control, MRP, BOM)?

Costing

The costing of manufactured goods can be carried out by a number of different methods. In one method, standards are set up at the beginning of a period and later compared to actual costs. In another, actual costs are gathered against specific jobs or contracts and these form the basis of the charge which is made to the customer for the product. Some systems require considerable time to be spent in their administration, while others can barely be called a system and proceed largely by rule-of-thumb methods. Given the importance to a manufacturing company of knowing what each product costs to make, with its implications for selling price and profitability, it is surprising how many of them do not know, appear to consider it of minor significance or delude themselves into thinking that they do know. In many cases this is almost certainly because of the perceived difficulty in administering effective costing systems. A costing module within an integrated CAPM system can make this task very much easier, provided the basic disciplines of data gathering are followed, and provide information on the finished products and manufacturing processes which, for example, can be used effectively to increase profitability on individual products or rationalize product ranges.

The type of costing system in use will largely be determined by the nature of the business, eg contract costing, and may well be in place in a manual mode or in a partly computerized format. In any event, a costing system within an integrated suite of CAPM programs will often provide data as a by-product of the Work-In-Process or Shopfloor Control module, insofar as data which is gathered and recorded for production purposes is used also for costing purposes without further manual intervention, eg productive hours expended and materials used on each works order. Once the costing files have been set up with overhead rates, labour rates, etc, this information will be used to calculate actual costs automatically, and if the system is so designed, to give comparisons with standard or estimated costs. Here are some of the main aspects of costing which should be considered.

Is the system to be of the last in, first out (LIFO), first in, first out (FIFO), 'average' or 'current' cost type? Is it to be for job, product or contract costing? In what way will labour hours need to be handled, eg set-up, production, re-work, idle time? What details on labour rates will be required? What methods will be most appropriate for the recording and calculation of material usage? How many overhead rates are in use and how are they applied? Are sub-contract costs an important component of total cost, and how are these to be handled? Will data be required to be drawn from a costed BOM? Will a cost simulation function be required? What interfaces would be required with other CAPM programs (eg BOMs, inventory control, shopfloor control, purchase order processing)?

Data volumes

The information gathered after detailed examination of all the relevant functions within the manufacturing organization will form the basis of the software systems specification. The other vital information which must be gathered is the data volumes. This consists of the volumes of transactions, records and documentation which the new systems will need to handle. The calculation of storage capacity required will normally be carried out by the systems vendor. Some of the data volumes may not be readily available and will require some work to determine, even to the extent of counting a year's worth of sales invoices for example, but the data is essential to the systems vendor. If you don't provide it in the specification he or she will only ask for it later or make an educated guess and fix the hardware price accordingly.

Surveying available CAPM packages

The foregoing sections give an indication of the kind of questions which must be asked in order that a suitable systems specification can be drawn up for submission to potential systems vendors. It is in no way comprehensive and is not intended to be, for to set out every possible parameter, to predict each and every question about all aspects of an integrated CAPM system would take up many more pages than can be devoted here to the subject. Many of the questions that need to be asked will be obvious, as they will arise from the everyday working of the present systems in your company. Others will result from a process of thought and deduction. Yet there is more that this required, because in order to get the right answers from suppliers, one must ask them the right questions, and these can only be put by someone with sufficient knowledge of what is commonly available in package CAPM programs. And in practical terms, this means one of two things. Either a consultant should have been engaged or someone from the company with a good working knowledge of its different functions should carry out a survey of available systems, ranging across the price and functionality spectra, to determine what is available and what the likely costs would be.

If the person from your company is starting from scratch – that is, with no knowledge of the CAPM market and its offerings – then the expense of acquiring such knowledge may amount to more than would pay for a consultant to do the job instead. There are companies who have tackled this question with significant success because they have picked the right internal people and given them the time and resources to carry out the project in a professional manner. It cannot be stressed too often that this is no place for the well-intentioned amateur with scant knowledge. In that direction lies expensive failure, or at best a poorly-implemented system which does not give the necessary return on capital invested. This applies not only to the systems specification but also for the next stage in the proceedings, the drawing up of a list of potential suppliers. If you want to spend many wasted hours on the telephone, be badgered by visiting salesmen and inundated with calls and literature on systems for every conceivable type of business from church administration to stock-breeding, then you could simply try calling some computer systems vendors from the 'phone book. Otherwise it should be approached a little more scientifically.

Some of the places where details of CAPM systems can be gleaned are:

- Magazines specializing in CAPM. Not only will these carry advertisements for a range of systems but they will, from time to time, conduct surveys of available systems, usually with some details of applications, functionality and price.

- Trade magazines, which may carry system advertisements, reviews of general or industry-specific CAPM systems and articles by users explaining the benefits and drawbacks of the systems which they have implemented.

- Other organizations of a similar type to your own, who have successfully implemented a CAPM system. A strong word of caution is required here, however. If it is the first fully integrated CAPM system to be seen by the steering committee, it is easy to be so enamoured with it that they almost decide on the spot that this is the one for your company and rush off to sign on the dotted line. The organization which shows it to you may not be entirely objective in their evaluation, as they are unlikely to admit that they were responsible for selecting a poor system which has brought them nothing but trouble.

- Enquiries made to the major hardware suppliers regarding 'third party software'; that is, CAPM systems which have been written to run on their equipment by software houses for whose competency they will vouch. Make them aware that you are only conducting a general survey.

- If a consultant has been engaged, it will be part of his or her function to provide a short list of likely suppliers, having already conducted a search of appropriate systems.
- Catalogues and databases of CAPM systems.
- Trade associations, if your industry is the type catered for by industry-specific packages, such as printing and shoemaking.

By this time, the steering committee should have some idea as to what size of budget would be available for purchase of the required hardware and software. This will be one of the major determining factors in the type of system chosen. Others will be the size of your company, what industry it is in, what main functions (eg inventory control, MRP, job costing) you will require of your new CAPM system. If there are any restrictions on the type of hardware on which the system should run or its operating system, then this also must be clearly defined. Finally, even at this early stage in the selection process, the key features, without which any system would be a non-starter, must be decided upon. Some examples of this might be lot traceability, contract costing, or the ability to interface, and the availability of financial accounts software which will support multi-currency transactions. Don't be too demanding: these must be essential to retaining the true character of your business. Neither should you cast your net so wide that every system you evaluate qualifies.

Drawing up a short list

The process consists of examining the various literature to see how many package CAPM systems match up with the main requirements which you have listed. Depending on how unusual your company requirements are, you will discover a match in numerous instances, a reasonable number to constitute a short list, or none at all. If the latter is the case, then the steering committee must then re-examine the stated requirements and question the reasoning behind each one. Have they been realistic in the budget that has been allowed? Do you need to start with a large system or could you implement a core suite of systems and add other modules later? Does some corporate policy really tie you to one type of hardware? Are you sure the CAPM system hardware will need the option of interfacing with the computer in R&D which does nothing but scientific calculations? Are those features really essential or simply ones which it would be nice to have?

Of course, it may be the case that, having re-examined and confirmed your main needs in a CAPM system, you still cannot find any that suit. This would then require a wider search to be instituted, using the same media as before. Failing all of this, then you will probably have only three options left: abandon the project, implement those package programs which are acceptable and have the remainder bespoke-written, or change some part of your requirements. The bespoke-writing of complete CAPM programs is very expensive and time-consuming. It produces software which is non-standard and expensive to maintain, and if the company that writes it ever goes out of business it can be extremely difficult to get anyone else to touch it. Such systems should be avoided if at all possible.

The short list of potential vendors which you select should number no more than four or five. It is tempting to include more, especially if many of them easily come within your initial broad requirements, but this should be avoided. Unless you are prepared to have someone devote a large amount of time to examining the tenders (often in excess of a hundred pages each) when they come in, and a group of people spending days at demonstrations and user visits, keep the shortlist to what it is supposed to be – short. If there is no preference for hardware or operating system then try and include a number of different options, eg mini-computer and networked (local or wide area network) systems. Unless your company is feeling adventurous, only select those software packages which have all programs currently available and have a reasonable number of users in existence. There can be certain advantages in breaking new ground, and these will be discussed in the next chapter. Generally speaking, it should be avoided.

When the steering committee is reasonably satisfied with the short list, each of the potential vendors should be contacted and given some idea of your requirements, any special features, the size of your company and so forth. Tell them that you intend to send them an ITT and ask them if they are willing to respond. If they ask you, as they often will, whether you have a budget for the project, tell them that the cost is not unimportant but that it takes second place to implementing the best system for your company. Inform them that a tight schedule has been drawn up and that you will need to receive their tender within three weeks of their date of receipt. A note to this effect should also be inserted in the ITT. This is not an unreasonable timescale. Some of them will reply within a fortnight and others will still take four to six weeks.

CHAPTER 7

Evaluation and Purchase

Evaluation of tenders

When the tenders are received from the potential systems vendors, they have to be compared to your company's requirements as set out in the systems specification and generally examined to ensure that what is being offered is clearly understood. Naturally, the first page to which most people will turn will be the one with the summary of costs on it. Don't be surprised if all of them are above your budget figure, some of them substantially so. If the research has been properly carried out before the list of potential vendors has been drawn up, then your budget is likely to be realistic. However, there are other costs besides hardware and software to be met and these may amount to a substantial increase on the basic price. For example, these extra costs could be for installation, training, implementation or cabling, and you can be sure that most vendors will not stint on their services when they make up the estimate. For now, let us ignore those large price tags and concentrate on the matters of initial importance: the degree of fit between the systems specification and the vendors' offerings.

The tenders which vendors submit when offering a CAPM system can range from a poorly-bound collection of pages in dot-matrix print which are in no way specific to the purchaser's requirements, to a number of huge ring binders, each page with the purchaser's logo on it, and including everything and more that one could ask. It is natural to expect that vendors with well-presented tenders will subsequently prove to be the most efficient in operation and the most caring about their customer. This is not always so. Like the later demonstrations by vendors, a slickly presented tender only proves one thing – that the vendor is good at presentation. Most of the better CAPM systems vendors are good at presentation; it's part of their job. It is your company's job to find out if there is any substance behind the façade.

New or established system

Assuming that you are interested in acquiring an integrated suite of CAPM packages – although all that will be said holds good for a single module or a small number of them – one of the first things which should be ascertained is whether or not all the software is currently available. This is not always as easy to find out as you might suppose, as some vendors will respond in the affirmative to requests for certain modules on the basis that they are planned for release in the near future. Unfortunately, the software vendor's concept of the near future does not always accord with that of the purchaser, and in any event, software houses are notorious for not keeping to program release dates. Also, if a program has not yet come on the market it cannot have been field tested and the bugs ironed out, and you should only take on the role of guinea-pig if you are quite clear as to what it will entail.

Companies whose CAPM systems requirements are unusual will obviously have a more restricted choice in package programs than those whose needs are fairly standard, so there may be little alternative but to take the available programs in a system, with the others to follow at given dates. Generally this is seen as a disadvantage, yet there can be some benefits from this course of action, provided that the bargaining is concluded before a contract is signed. These might be:

- your company can influence the design of programs
- you can negotiate a significant reduction in the purchase price because your company will be used as a test-bed
- your company will benefit from considerable implementation assistance free-of-charge from the vendor because it is the first implementation of one or more programs
- your company may be first in the field with an innovative system which would put you ahead of your competitors.

There may also be the possibility of gaining a further price reduction if you can get the vendor to accept you as a reference site to which other potential purchasers will be brought once your systems are fully operational. All of this would be quite apart from the normal price negotiations which should significantly reduce the figure first quoted in the tender document.

Detailed comparison of functionality and features

To ensure that no detail of the tenders is missed, each one needs to be scrutinized line by line. For medium-sized systems requirements, a minimum of a day should be allowed for each tender, with extra time for writing the report and tenders summary. It will be of considerable assistance if you have stated in your systems specification that each tendering company should include with its tender a list of your systems requirements, suitably marked to indicate the availability of each feature. Otherwise the task of matching the specification to the tender document, much of which will be in a pre-determined format, will be even more time-consuming. You might even fail to find any reference in the vendor's literature to some of the features you have listed and have to contact him or her for further information. If you receive assurances that the software will perform as you wish on specific points which are not made clear in the tender, have the software vendor confirm this in writing. It won't necessarily be a legally binding document but it will enable you to bring some considerable moral pressure to bear if things go awry.

Almost anything is possible if you fling enough money at the problem, and it sometimes appears that some software vendors have this adage in mind when preparing tenders for CAPM systems. There is no problem. Their system will do all of those things that you require. It is only later that the provisos are heard: " . . . as long as we change this bit and add on a bit here", or " . . . once we've got the front-end of the sales order processing system written". Before any decision is made, all aspects of the proposed system must be quite clear and unequivocal. To reiterate a point made above and add two others:

- all programs must be available at the time of purchase
- they must be complete and fully tested
- all the interfaces between programs must be operational

It would do no harm to include conditions such as these in the systems specification.

What is more difficult to detect, and where the expert knowledge of the consultant is invaluable, is where a certain feature is requested and assurances are given by the vendor that it is within the capability of the program in question, but where the program does not truly have that function in it and can only provide some of its elements. Supplemented by manual procedures, an approximation of the required function can be achieved but it will likely be cumbersome to operate and will not be as good as a system which has been purpose written. As an example, a measure of batch traceability can sometimes be achieved by the use of elaborate manual and computer systems. Nevertheless, the system cannot be said to have a batch traceability function. If you are prepared to settle for something like this, so be it, but do make sure you are not paying for a feature which in fact will mainly be provided by manual methods. It is not always enough simply to ask 'Will your system provide this function?' In what manner it provides that function can also be of great importance.

As has been said, the main work of the evaluation process is the detailed comparison of your systems specification with the replies received from vendors. Either through the check-list which has been supplied or by painstaking examination of the tender, it is established which features are available in each program. Do not simply set aside unread any tender which quotes a price well above the computerization project budget. Unlikely as it may appear at the time, such systems may well come back into the reckoning at a later stage. The next step is to calculate the degree of fit of the various package systems on offer, and this can be done in a number of ways.

Ranking

It may be that everything required is available in a particular system and that concentration would then be on other aspects of that offering. This will rarely be the case. A simple method of assessment is merely to count the total number of features/functions specified and express this as a percentage of the number available. However, this fails to take account of the relative importance of the different requirements. As previously mentioned, requirements should be ranked in some way and weightings given to each category. There is no need to be elaborate here. A simple system such as that described earlier should suffice. You will notice that there is no mention of an essential category, as any system without the essentials would normally be a non-starter. Dependent on circumstances, there may be exceptions to this rule. If the price of a software system containing one or more 'essential' feature is unacceptably high, then a decision may have to be made to accept one without this capability and carry out this procedure in a manual or semi-manual mode. This can occur where a small company with a restricted data processing budget uses sophisticated systems, eg a defence contractor, with requirements for batch and serial number traceability, contract costing and quality assurance.

When the features and functions present in a system have been identified from the tender document, they should be placed in the categories E, N, D or M. E is for essential and any element thus designated will have no marks given to it. The other three are given their appropriate values and the points added, the total being expressed as a percentage of the total points possible. If necessary, a percentage fit for each of the software programs within the system can also be calculated. At this stage there is no need to take particular note of, or make allowances in, the weightings for those functions which can only be provided by 'tailoring' standard systems at extra cost. This cost should be included in the total price when the packages are compared and it will mitigate against it. The results from each tender can then be compared and given in the report on systems selection, which will be explained later in this chapter.

Key points in the tender

As well as the software systems, points can be awarded to each of the answers to the questions in the general section at the front of the Invitation to Tender (ITT) (Appendix I), although this is more difficult to do fairly, as they cannot always produce a simple 'yes' or 'no' answer. The evaluation of this part of the response is nevertheless extremely important, and some points need to be highlighted.

Hardware

One matter of major importance with regard to hardware is its capability for expansion, by the addition of extra terminals, without the need to change the central processing unit (CPU). An indication of terminal requirements should have been given in the specification, and this figure must include an estimate of the total number expected to be operational at the end of, say, five years. The hardware which is finally chosen should be capable of supporting at least 50 per cent more terminals than this, to allow for unforseen expansion and to ensure that the systems' response times do not slow down excessively because of heavy usage. Care should also be taken to ensure that the cost of upgrading the CPU (replacing it or adding an expansion board or disk capacity), is clearly stated by the potential vendor in writing. In neglecting these aspects of hardware acquisition, a number of companies have later found their capacity to expand the system only possible at considerable extra expense.

Operating software

Operating software is not always treated by prospective purchasers with the attention it deserves. Unlike the hardware and the output from the applications software, the operating system is largely unseen as it works away in the background, controlling access to the computer files, moving data from one location to the other and managing various elements of the system such as programs, printers and memory. It could be said that in many cases the operating system under which the applications software runs is fairly irrelevant, as long as it is efficient in operation, and this would be substantially true as far as the average CAPM package system is concerned. However, a number of CAPM systems will only run under one operating system, although some will run under any one of three or four. There are a considerable number of operating systems in existence and, as with the applications software, it generally makes sense to choose one

which is well tried and in widespread use, such as UNIX, PICK, VMS or MS-DOS, provided of course that the applications programs you want can be run on it. The question of your systems' compatibility with other systems which you might already have installed or could implement in the future is also important and should be checked with the vendor. All other things being equal, the priorities which should be followed when evaluating a CAPM system should be:
1. applications software
2. operating software
3. hardware.

Applications software

As can be seen from Appendix I, there are quite a number of questions which should be asked of the potential vendor regarding the applications software which he or she is offering. As well as degree of fit to your requirements, the extent of any tailoring necessary and the price to be charged, it is important to establish things like the number of systems in use and the quality of support available after implementation. It may also be important for your organization to have access to the source code, if it is available from the vendor, when changes are planned to the programs. This is something which is often requested by the Data Processing Departments of companies implementing CAPM or other package programs. Though this facility may at times be useful, it is generally the case that it is unnecessary and even dangerous to adapt programs in this way. Any tailoring which is required is best carried out by the vendor. If major work is thought to be required at the outset, then perhaps the wrong suite of programs has been chosen. Some organizations say that they wish to have the source code in case amendments are needed to the program at a later date, or to safeguard their interests if the vendor should ever go out of business. In the first instance, this should also be carried out by the vendor, so that the programs remain standard, or at least compatible with any system updates which are brought out. In the second instance, any reputable vendor should have copies of the source code permanently deposited with some institution such as a bank, to ensure that whatever happens, users' systems can be maintained.

Maintenance

Adequate maintenance of both software and hardware is of vital importance to any organization whose business relies so heavily on it as does that of the average CAPM user. If the whole system crashes, or even a part of it ceases to function properly, the company's day-to-day operations may well grind to a halt, with untold expense being incurred. The amount of lost time experienced by users of reputable hardware and software is usually very small, but it can still be devastating when it occurs. The questions to which you require answers are, What will be done about it if it does happen? By whom? How fast? And at what cost? Those companies who are so reliant on their computer systems that they are not prepared to accept the possibility of any hardware breakdown whatsoever go to the extent and major expense of installing a duplicate computer. Few companies could justify this expense and therefore it makes sense to ensure that whatever maintenance agreement you accept, it is sufficient for your needs and represents value for money.

Training and implementation

The amount and quality of training offered in the use of CAPM systems can vary greatly from one vendor to another and you should find out its extent and price before making any firm commitment to purchase the system. The vendor must specify how many man-days training are included and what the cost of extra days would be. Is the tuition to take place at his or her premises or can it be carried out at yours? Is there any responsibility placed on the vendor to ensure that those who have to operate the systems will achieve a certain level of competence within a given time?

Using data from your own organization, practical training at the keyboard for everyone in attendance must be given, and not simply lectures by vendor personnel. In addition to operator education and training there should also be made provision for those who will not operate the systems but will supervise those who do and those who simply use its output. Middle and senior management must also be given an appreciation of how the systems work and the range of their abilities.

Contractual terms

These can deal with many different aspects of the proposed systems, their acquisition, usage and disposal. They would normally be scrutinized, prior to signature, by the Company Secretary or lawyer to ensure that they were legally sound. There are nevertheless a number of other aspects which need to be considered and which should be made clear in the sample contract which the vendor should provide as an appendix to his or her tender document. The contractual policy on systems acceptance tests should be given, along with those on price revisions, delivery dates of both hardware and software (an area fraught with danger if care is not taken), and other items such as system enhancements and trade-in policy and terms. This last one is especially important if it is your organization's intention to purchase and run a small system for some time, perhaps for familiarization purposes, and then trade it in for a larger one.

System sizing

The volume data given at the end of the systems specification (Appendix I) will be used by the vendor to calculate the storage capacity required in your proposed computer system. This will directly determine the disk size in your CPU, the model of computer which is being offered and the capacity in the individual terminals if a network system is being offered. This of course will have a major bearing on the price of the hardware. Assurances should be sought and obtained, in writing, from the vendor that the storage capacity proposed in the tender will be adequate for estimated future needs – enough to cater for the next five years plus 50 per cent. It is unfortunately the case that some systems vendors, large and prestigious as well as small, can resort to unethical means to try and win the contract, by deliberately undersizing the system by a significant amount and thereby keeping the price low. They know that it will be some considerable time before the lack of capacity becomes apparent, and you can be sure that they will have some plausible argument as to why you need to trade in your present CPU (on very favourable terms) and buy a larger one. If you have not employed a consultant to evaluate the tenders and make recommendations, you will need to compare the capacity of the different systems given in the tenders, and through discussions with the vendors assure yourself that adequate capacity has been allowed.

Report on the tenders

The person or persons charged with carrying out the vetting of tenders, whether consultant, project leader or members of the steering committee, should prepare a report on the tenders received for the chief executive officer and other decision-makers. This should be kept fairly brief since there is no merit in swamping people with masses of facts and figures which can be digested much more easily in summary form. The object of such a report is threefold:
1. To consider each offering in turn and explain its main strengths and weaknesses.
2. To make comparisons and draw conclusions as to the most suitable CAPM systems (if any) for the organization's needs.
3. To analyse the financial aspects of each tender and give a cost justification for those systems recommended.

In the first instance, some details of the tendering company should be given, with an indication of its reputation, number of systems in operation and years in existence. To what extent the tender meets with the requirements in the specification, and the implications for the company's present methods of operation must then be clearly demonstrated, albeit in summary form. Other important aspects should also be included, where appropriate, such as the suitability of the proposed hardware and the operating system. In comparing the various elements of the applications software for functionality and general fitness of purpose it should be remembered that not all systems achieve similar goals in the same way, therefore it is not always enough to know what is achieved but also how it is achieved. This will ensure that the proposed systems will conform to the present methods of working in a particular function, or make clear what changes would be required in those functions if the system in question was to be implemented.

Financial analysis

The costs (or 'investment' as it is often termed by the computer vendors) which are given in the tender documents do not conform to a set pattern. This can make it difficult to compare like with like during the evaluation process. Some costs will be laid out in the greatest of detail – the price of each type of printer, the number of days training and the daily rate, item by item, costs for hardware and software maintenance. Other suppliers will merely give summary costs for such elements as hardware, software, training and implementation 'support'. In some tenders, all of the likely costs will not be included and will have to be requested from the vendor or estimated by the evaluator. Those costs which are included may be buried somewhere in the text, and it is not always clear whether they are in addition to, or a duplicate of, some of the figures given in the 'investment' section of the tender. All cost figures given in all the tender documents under consideration should be extracted and, insofar as is possible, laid out in a set format. It is not critical exactly what form this takes, as long as it covers all elements of cost. An example of a simple format is given in Appendix II, in which costs are grouped under headings such as CPU, printers, visual display units (VDUs), training and cabling. The cost of each module of application software should also be entered, if available, so that differences in price between vendors can be highlighted. The costs given in the tender costs should then be incorporated into the summary (Appendix III), which gives a good financial overview of all the tenders received and makes them easy to compare both in part and in total. The final column shows the total capital and maintenance costs that will be incurred, averaged over a five-year period. This is intended only as a guide for the purpose of comparing the costs of the different CAPM systems submitted. If required, a detailed cost/benefit analysis for one or more systems may be carried out by a financial accountant.

The financial appraisal technique to be used will depend on the convention within your organization. The reason for any such financial appraisal is to determine whether net cash inflows over a given period are sufficiently higher than net outflows. Of course, there may be other reasons for implementing a CAPM system, or parts of it, such as compatibility with other companies in a group or the ability to interface with a customer's systems. These may not be justifiable on the grounds of internal efficiency, but their financial benefit may arise from increased sales, and they should certainly be looked at from the point of view of what financial losses are likely to be incurred if the systems are not implemented.

Some organizations seem to be happy with a simple form of financial appraisal, showing the cash inflows and outflows over a period of time. Others require something more sophisticated and use one of the techniques given below or a variant of it.

Payback: This is a method of estimating the time it will take for the flow of cash receipts to pay back the initial investment, but it will not show any profits which occur following the completion of the payback period.

Rate of return: This is a fairly crude method which does not take any account of the timings of the return. There are a number of variations on this method, one of which is the expected profit, less depreciation, expressed as a percentage of the capital invested.

Net present value: Starting with a given rate of interest, this method calculates the amount of the present value of future flows of income from an investment, whereas discounted cash flow (a variant of the same principle) calculates the rate of return.

Whatever method of appraisal is used, the result will need to be included in the report on the chosen system which will be drawn up by the consultant or the project leader. If comprehensive justification is part of your company's capital requisition procedures then a separate report may not be required, but it is often advisable to include a short report which includes the salient facts about the proposed project, and a well-argued case for its implementation. Its acceptance by the board of directors may depend on it.

The final selection

The steering committee will be the body responsible for putting forward recommendations to the chief executive officer and the board of directors, based on the report which has evaluated the operational and financial aspects of each CAPM program considered. As described, points should have been awarded according to the category of each feature in the specification and the resulting total from each tender expressed as a percentage of available points. A cost/benefit analysis will have shown whether or not the investment in hardware, software and ancillary services is acceptable to your organization. From the four or five packages which made up the original list, two at most need to be selected for more detailed scrutiny. If for one reason or another none of those evaluated are acceptable, another batch of the many CAPM packages on the market will need to be picked and the tender and evaluation process gone through once more, although this is unlikely to be necessary if the original group has been chosen with care.

Assuming that the steering committee has narrowed the original choice of systems down to two or three, the next step is to arrange demonstrations of the systems, set up visits to user sites and obtain a list of current system users which should be supplied by the respective vendors. A list of just a few names is hardly satisfactory as they may have been carefully selected to exclude any implementations which have not been a success. Up to half a dozen names should be picked at random from such a list and a telephone call made to the manufacturing manager or equivalent in each company to seek opinion of the system that was installed and the level of implementation assistance and maintenance service given by the systems vendor. Of course, this method is not foolproof, as a person will not readily admit to their CAPM system selection and implementation having been an unmitigated disaster. Conversations with current systems users will give you a general idea in what regard the vendor is held by his customers and may elicit a few tips which will save you time and effort at a later stage. Comments can range from the "It's a fantastic system, the answer to all our problems" variety, to "It cannot do proper contract costing like they said it would, and 18 months later we are still waiting on the program to be adapted to suit our requirements."

If nothing arises to deter you from dealing with the two or three vendors on the short list, it is now time to arrange for a demonstration of each system. This would normally be carried out at the vendor's premises, where he or she will have appropriate hardware on which to run it, although it may be possible for the system to be demonstrated at your premises if the hardware is portable or the programs can be run on your own hardware. The object of a demonstration is to allow as many of the steering committee or users as possible to scrutinize, in working mode, all of the programs which are under consideration and to question those demonstrating the system about functionality and methods of operation. It is preferable if data from your own organization is used, depending on its suitability to the system and the time available to set it up. However comprehensive, a mere 'run through' the system, with the various features and functions being pointed out, is not sufficient. In order that those evaluating the system can fully appreciate how it operates, worked examples should be given, eg receiving a sales order, raising a works order, drawing up a bill of materials and a manufacturing route, scheduling the job through production and recording costs and performance. Insofar as it is possible, demonstrations should be given and assurances obtained that the system can give those key features required in an acceptable manner. Examples of output documents from the system should also be made available. A full day, or longer if need be, should be set aside for each system demonstration.

The demonstration having proved satisfactory (and it is following unsatisfactory demonstrations that many systems are dropped from short lists), a visit to one or more user sites should be undertaken. It is best if you are able to pick an organization at random from a list of users, but this is not often possible, and for good reason. Some companies are not keen to have outsiders going round their plant, possibly disrupting operations and scrutinizing their manufacturing methods. The very companies which would be most appropriate for you to visit, those in the same business, are exactly the ones which would not want to let a competitor inside the front door. This is unfortunate but understandable. Normally you will have to settle for a visit to a company which is similar in size and manufacturing systems requirements to your own. Often, the number of personnel they will allow to visit is restricted and may not be sufficient to accomodate all those from your organization who wish to attend.

Having said all of this, there is no doubt that an appropriate site visit is very useful, if not essential, in evaluating a shortlisted CAPM system. There is the opportunity for personnel from your company to talk to their counterparts who will be systems users of some months or years experience, the system can be seen working in a manufacturing environment, and opinions as to its effectiveness and ease of use can be obtained. The enquiries made on these user visits should cover the following key points:

- the quality of training and implementation assistance provided by the system vendor
- the vendor adherence to agreed delivery dates for hardware and software, especially for software 'tailoring'
- ease of use of the systems, including the instructional documentation
- system functionality in operation, as opposed to claims made by the vendor
- the actual total cost of the implementation compared with the estimated cost, and details of any major variances

There may also be general questions about their system implementation which can be asked, eg Did any major and unexpected problems arise, and has the system given the increased efficiency and return on investment originally envisaged? A number of CAPM package systems have user associations, details of which would normally be given by the vendor following purchase. If you can speak to some members of the user association during your evaluation process, so much the better.

CHAPTER 8

Project Planning

One of the keys to the successful implementation of a CAPM system is good project planning. Too often a project fails to achieve its objectives, the resources required turn out to have been grossly under-estimated or the project takes much longer than anticipated because inadequate thought and time were given to this aspect of the project. There is nothing magical about the technique of project planning. It does not have to be sophisticated, but it must be comprehensive in that all actions or tasks to be performed in order to effect the implementation must be planned over the life of the project, and the resources of manpower (and cost, if required) calculated. This plan must be realistic and achievable from those resources that are known to be available. It must be compared continually against what is actually happening and adapted where necessary so that it always shows the real status of the project and not a rose-tinted picture of how it should be. The project plan is the primary tool for the planning and monitoring of every element of the implementation.

The outline plan

An outline project plan should be drawn up as early as possible and should show the estimated timescales for all of the major activities. There are a number of techniques available; the most common one, and the one which will be used here, being based on the Gannt Chart principle in which time is shown on the horizontal plane and activities listed on the perpendicular. The outline plan can be used initially to determine the overall timescale and the sequence of events within it, later to be developed into a full-blown implementation plan. A section of such an outline plan is given below.

CAPM PROJECT.		XYZ CO LTD					
Activity	Jan	Feb	Mar	Apr	May	June	July
Feasibility	*******						
Specification		****					
Selection			***				
Training				***			
Data preparation			***************				
Delivery					**		
Data entry					*****		
Inventory control						****	
BOM							****
Routeing							****

The outline plan can only be drawn up with the assistance of the steering committee who, collectively representing all the interested functions within the company, have the best knowledge of what is practical and desirable. In determining the global timescale, one must take into consideration the present state of the organization's systems and methods of working. Transferring from one CAPM system to another, where data integrity is high and systems discipline good, is a different matter entirely from introducing CAPM to a company where poor record keeping, taking shortcuts with the system and lack of accountability is the order of the day. How accurate are the bills of material and routings and how long will it take to make them suitable for a CAPM system? How accurate are inventory records? What time can be devoted to preparation for CAPM?

In practice, it is often the case that an arbitrary future date is picked for the completion of the CAPM system implementation, on the basis that it should take about a year to 18 months to achieve. If a consultant has been retained, he or she will be able to estimate quite accurately the time that should be allowed, based on experience of other implementations and knowledge of the areas in which difficulties often arise. The implementation of a fully-integrated CAPM system can of course be compressed into a short time or lengthened to cover many months, and there can be valid reasons for each approach. But generally speaking, the aim should be to maintain a brisk pace, neither taking things so slowly that interest and momentum are lost or pushing the pace so much that people fall by the wayside exhausted. In a small to medium-sized manufacturing plant with reasonably good systems in place, a year would be an acceptable implementation time, from commencement of the feasibility study until the whole system is fully operational. Some systems have been successfully implemented in a much shorter time, and this is generally the result of good planning and availability of adequate resources.

The detailed plan

The responsibility for drawing up the detailed plan (see Figure 8.1), maintaining it and keeping participants informed of progress should be given to one person, most likely the project leader or the consultant. It must be accepted from the outset that the plan is not something that will be drawn up once and will not subsequently change. Some target dates will have to be put back because of unforseen events or early misjudgements as to the levels of resource required for a specific activity. Certain tasks may prove easier than expected and can be completed early. There may be delays in hardware and software delivery or bugs in a program which are difficult to find. All of these things and more will require plan changes which will in turn have effects on other tasks and activities and may effect the final completion date.

Any planning method used must therefore be flexible enough to accommodate such changes easily and quickly reproduce copies of the updated version for distribution to all of those involved. Various manual methods of planning for projects of this size and larger have been in use for hundreds of years, ranging from a simple list of sequential activities to complex systems of critical path analysis. The use of such manual systems is still widespread and many of them have proven their effectiveness over the years. But for large and multi-faceted projects they are difficult to set up and maintain and are rapidly being replaced by computerized systems which are inexpensive both to purchase and to use. There are a number of such systems now available and, given the importance of project planning for a CAPM implementation, it is well worth making the modest investment to acquire one, even if it would be of no further use after project completion.

There are two main methods of implementing any CAPM system, all of which are made up of various application software programs or modules. One is to have the whole integrated system go 'live' at one time, perhaps having been preceded by parallel running with the old system. The other and more common method is to implement the system in stages and ensure that each group of sub-systems is running satisfactorily before proceeding to the next one. The first method has little to recommend it. It can, rarely, be a dramatic success, with benefits immediately apparent on all fronts. But it often turns out to be a 'sink or swim' method, with a high rate of return but a very high risk factor. Unless a simultaneous implementation is essential, the

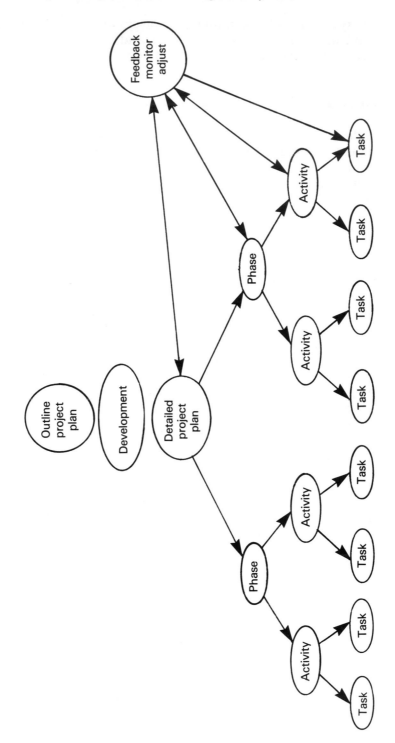

Figure 8.1 *Project planning*

CAPM system should be introduced in a series of steps, each one building wholly or partially on what has gone before.

The main elements of the project plan will be the same, regardless of the sequence of module implementation. These are planning, implementation and post-implementation and can be sub-divided into specific activities as shown below, in the sequence in which they are likely to occur.

Planning

Appoint steering committee	Assessment of tenders
CAPM education	Report and short list
Draw up project plan	Systems demonstrations
Feasibility study and report	Visits to user sites
Draw up specification	System selection
Approve specification	Capital approval
Submit invitation to tender (ITT)	Place order for CAPM system

This section would be concluded with a review of the manufacturing systems currently in operation at the company to determine the interfaces with the new CAPM system. The present organizational structure and staffing levels would also need to be examined to determine what changes if any would need to be effected. These will be treated more fully in a later chapter, as will the sequence of software module implementation, the sequence given below being arbitrary and for explanatory purposes only.

Implementation

Preparation I

Data Check – BOM	Decide document formats
– Purchase orders	Order stationery
– Sales orders	Site survey
– Inventory	

As some time will elapse between placing the order for the CAPM system and taking delivery, the checking of data already on file and the creation of new data where necessary, can take place provided that adequate training has been given on the format and content of data for input to the CAPM system files.

Delivery and installation

Site preparation	Hardware Set-up and test
Cabling	Software set-up and test
Hardware delivery	System commissioning
Software delivery	

Education and training I

Systems overview	Inventory control

BOM   Sales order processing
Purchase order processing

The initial education will give an overview of the whole CAPM system, both for users and management, explaining the principles on which it is based and showing the relationships between the different modules. The subsequent training in each module will be for users.

Systems set-up I
Systems parameters   Customer files
Parts master files   Purchase order files
Supplier files   Sales order files
BOM files

Data entry I
Inventory   Purchase orders
Supplier   Sales orders
Customer   BOM

When all of the current and historical data has been entered into the computer files, the modules can be run for a trial period. When this proves successful, live running can follow. The groups of activities listed above, with the exception of Delivery and Install, will then be repeated for each of the remaining implementation phases, eg production control, MRP, costing and estimating, until the whole CAPM system is live and fully integrated. Interspersed with all of the activities listed above should be planned steering committee meetings at about two-week intervals, at which progress will be reviewed, tasks allocated and replanning carried out where necessary. Current computerized project planning systems have a number of sophisticated features which are of great value in the control of any sizeable implementation.

Post-implementation

Once the whole system has been running for a reasonable period of time, say three months, it should be thoroughly reviewed to ensure that the software is working in the expected manner and is being used properly and effectively. This is especially important for the remaining manual systems and their interfaces with the new computer ones. A report on the results of the review should be produced by the project leader and work carried out as early as possible, by retraining of users or redesigning manual/computer interfaces to rectify any shortcomings discovered.

The project plan for CAPM implementation should be at least as detailed in terms of activities or tasks as that given above and in the more detailed example in Appendix IV. Anything less will be inadequate for full control of the project. Various formats are possible, but they should all have the following elements:

- Activities listed sequentially
- The duration of each activity represented both numerically and graphically against a dated timescale
- The individuals responsible for execution of each activity
- The manpower required to carry out each activity.

Other features can be added if desired, such as the cost of manpower or a critical path analysis.

Activities and responsibilities

One of the roles of the project leader and the steering committee is to decide who should carry out each activity listed on the project plan and in each case choose an individual who will be given authority and have the responsibility for its completion. Some activities or tasks can be carried out by one person and some will require a team effort, but in every instance the responsibility must lie with a named individual who reports progress to the project leader. Designating a department or section without naming a leader (which may or may not be the normal section head) will more than likely result in failure to complete the task on time, with everyone disclaiming responsibility. Many of the jobs to be done by internal personnel will require considerable knowledge and skill, and as such will themselves suggest the most appropriate people to do them. Other tasks must be allocated on an equitable basis, dependent on the degree of effort required, the resources available and the benefits which will accrue to that department.

The time allowed for each activity or task is more problematic. The majority of organizations will not have tackled most of the activities needed for a CAPM implementation and will therefore have little basis on which to calculate the time required. How long will it take to go through every manufacturing routing on file and check its completeness and accuracy against present shopfloor practice? What actions are involved in entering data into the parts master files and who should do it – personnel who are knowledgeable about the technicalities of company inventory but have poor keyboard skills, or data entry clerks brought in temporarily for this task? Some estimate must be made for each activity so that it can be included in the plan, and these estimates can only come from those who know the present systems and the manner in which records are kept, eg the Purchasing Department for vendor records, the Process Planning Department for manufacturing routings. Significant, even radical, changes may have to be made to the original estimates as activities are begun and their true nature emerges, though estimates based on some research should mostly avoid this. Estimates based on figures "plucked out of thin air" are no more use in this situation than they are in any other.

At an early stage it should be made plain by the project leader to everyone concerned that the CAPM implementation will be the

second most important aspect of their work (after the normal duties of running the business), that the plan is not merely a guide or a faint hope but a set of instructions aimed at an achievable target and that no effort must be spared to complete each activity with accuracy and on time. Responsibilities are to be allocated to individuals and they will be held to them, with results being closely monitored through a predetermined chain of command, which may accord with the normal organization or may have been devised solely for the purposes of the project. More than enough problems will arise in any event, without these being exacerbated by misunderstandings about the project plan and its importance to the implementation.

Key targets

Although it does not relate directly to the subject of project planning, this is a convenient time to examine the setting of key performance targets. It is upon these that the whole premise of the CAPM implementation has been (or should have been) based. Many CAPM systems are implemented without performance targets being set or monitored, so that subsequent financial justification for the project is non-existent. What is the chief executive to say two years after the new system is operational when asked "What objectives was the expenditure of this large sum of money intended to achieve, and was it successful? In what way is your business better off than it was before you implemented CAPM?" Unfortunately, there are too few chief executives who would be in a position to answer with precise facts and figures.

The key targets against which the subsequent performance of the manufacturing operation will be measured should be made available along with the project plan to all steering committee members and managers. Managers in turn should make all of their personnel aware of these targets, both in corporate terms and in relation to each person's section or department. The project plan will require substantial extra effort from all of them and it is appropriate that the potential benefits are shown at the same time. And what should the key targets be? The answer to this must lie in the main with the potential benefits envisaged at the time of the financial justification or cost/benefit analysis of the project.

The sole reason for any capital expenditure in a commercial enterprise is to increase profits. While it may go under a variety of names or descriptions, larger profits are the target, whether through increased revenue or decreased costs. It may be unfortunate that businesses are assessed solely in a financial manner (how do you show high or low morale on the balance sheet?), yet until someone comes up with a better system we must work with the one we have. That is why anything which cannot be quantified financially should not be put down as a potential benefit from the CAPM system implementation. There is no way of making valid comparisons. Many targets can be set, from corporate ones of increased sales and profits to those at departmental level, such as reduced stock-outs of raw materials or lower machine downtime, although care should be taken to keep these to a minimum. Two, or at most three targets at any one time should suffice for each function.

The following are some of the targets which companies commonly attempt to achieve through investment in CAPM:

- Permanent reduction in raw materials stock and therefore in its holding costs through more efficient inventory control.
- Improved purchasing methods, resulting in better quality materials (less scrap/downtime) and lower unit costs.
- Improved sales order processing methods to give better response and improved product availability to customers, and therefore increase sales.
- More accurate BOM and routing data to reduce lost time in the production process and increase efficiency.
- Improved capacity planning and scheduling of production operations to reduce costs through better labour and machine utilization.
- Improved control of shopfloor operations resulting in the reduction of work-in-process.
- Accurate and timely reporting of manufacturing costs, to allow true costs to be known and remedial action to be taken (eg cost reduction, price increase, removal from product range).
- Permanent reduction in finished goods inventory without loss of availability, and subsequent lowering of holding costs.

Whatever the key targets, they should be quantifiable in units, money or percentages. Vague statements like 'greater efficiency', 'improved accuracy' or 'better customer relations' are inadequate as they are incapable of measurement and are open to different interpretations. The setting of targets and the monitoring of performance against them implies that the present levels of performance in the chosen areas can be accurately reported. This should be checked before firm targets are set. It may be necessary to devise and use exceptional methods of data gathering and reporting for the purpose of comparison with the later results from the CAPM system, especially so if a prime reason for implementing the new system is that the present one gives poor performance and cost information.

Each department or section implementing a module of the CAPM system should have at least one key target to reach, which it has helped to set. Each one will have a terminal status, for example 98 per cent accuracy in all BOM (ie 98 per cent of all BOM are 100 per cent accurate), reached by a series of steps which may be spread over the duration of the whole CAPM system implementation or over a shorter period. These targets should be clearly understood by those attempting to achieve them, ambitious but capable of attainment with given resources and the degree of achievement able to be easily measured. It will be part of the project manager's work to monitor all such targets, make regular verbal reports to the steering committee and include the performance figures in his or her periodic written reports to the chief executive officer and senior management.

CHAPTER 9

Education and Training

Of those CAPM systems which are badly implemented and fail to give the planned return on investment, a high proportion of them will be found to suffer, *inter alia,* from poor education and training of company personnel. A manufacturing organization may spend a considerable amount of money on systems selection (although this is often an area in which money is 'saved'), and on hardware and software, only to jeopardize the whole undertaking by skimping on the learning process. People at all levels in the organization, some of whom have barely grasped the concept of CAPM, are catapulted into new systems which will not only have a profound effect on their working methods but may also affect the nature and scope of each person's job. When there is surprise on the part of senior management that things did not go according to plan, blame is placed on those who apparently failed to make the system work. This is surely the wrong way to approach the subject.

If CAPM systems are to be successfully implemented and operated – and senior management have a duty to see that this is so – then not only are good education and training desirable but they are essential. They are not cheap, and some companies might see them as the straw that breaks the camel's back, after having to accept a higher-than-expected systems price; but they should be cost effective. There is an adage, "If you think training is expensive, then try doing without it", which is entirely appropriate in the case of CAPM implementation. There must be a commitment right from the start of the project, if necessary even before the decision is made to conduct a feasibility study, to undertake the best education and training available. This should be so even if it means settling for a cheaper system with less functionality than required so that the surplus money can be used on training. Money invested in relevant training is always well spent, yet there are often those with influence in a company who will say otherwise, and their opinions must not be allowed to prevail.

The education and training processes should take place at all levels within the company, at various times and using different methods. In the main, each sector within the company has different needs and should be treated accordingly.

Education

In this context, education is the process of learning the principles of CAPM systems, initially required by senior management in order that they might make informed judgements and decisions as to suitability for their manufacturing operations. CAPM education will also be required by those who are going to operate the systems so that they will be able to appreciate the reasoning behind them and see their work in the proper context. When should education commence? The easy answer to this would be "As soon as possible", but that doesn't get us very far. There will surely have been some level of CAPM knowledge within the company for the subject to have been raised. If adequate interest is generated amongst senior management then one or two persons can be delegated to attend a short (one- or two-day) appreciation course and to report back to their management committee or board of directors with their initial impressions of how CAPM might (or might not) serve their organization's needs. What should not be done at the early stage is to send anyone without CAPM knowledge to 'have a look' at systems vendors' demonstrations. This will only lead to confusion, as there will be no yardstick against which to measure the systems demonstrated.

The next step in the education process is for all executive officers and senior management of the company to attend a seminar of half-day duration. The objective of this is to explain CAPM and to sell the idea to the decision-makers, although you must be prepared for it to do the opposite. It is very tempting to hold the seminar on company premises because all senior people cannot be absent from the site at once. This should be resisted. The subject matter will have more impact if delivered in an external venue, even if only a mile down the road at the local hotel conference suite. If it is impossible to have everyone away at once then run two sessions, morning and afternoon.

This is a very important, though often neglected, part of the CAPM selection and implementation process, not only because some of these people will ultimately have to vote the money for the project but because they must become involved at an early stage and stay involved right through the life of the project. It is essential that senior management are seen to be involved. All too often they only become involved when expenditure is to be discussed and the rest of the time they leave middle management to run the project. Being a generic term, CAPM may not have the status of a 'philosophy' (rather than simply a production system) such as is claimed for JIT, yet to succeed it requires the same high level of continuous commitment and it must pervade every level of the manufacturing organization. Once those senior people are on the side of CAPM, keep them there by regular updates on progress, demonstrations of newly-installed modules, and regular reports of improvements made through its use. When the going gets tough, and little of the systems implementation seems to be going right, it will need their support.

If an external consultant is used in the selection and implementation processes, then not only should he or she have the required technical knowledge, he should also be capable of undertaking the various education seminars required. When a person from your own organization is seconded to carry out these tasks, he or she may need a considerable amount of education, unless having previously gained experience at another company. One possibility is to seek out someone with good experience of CAPM selection and implementation and employ them on a full-time basis. He or she will be able to bring the necessary knowledge into the organization, manage the whole selection and implementation project and then remain permanently in the company to run the system. This would of course depend on a number of factors, not least the size of the system and how cost-effective such a tactic would be. For the medium- to large-sized organization it is certainly worth considering.

Companies often ask why any external help from consultants or trainers is needed, why further expense should be incurred for education and training. Isn't that what the systems vendor is supposed to do? The systems vendor will certainly provide training in the use of his own software (beware the exceptions), but such organizations are rarely able to offer education in the principles and practice of CAPM or advice on the human aspects of the project. Nor will they be concerned with the manual systems which must remain and interface with the computer ones. They will tell you what documentation can be produced by their software, but they cannot say when it should be produced, who should receive it and what should be done with it. CAPM is just as much about people as it is about computer software, and the implementation of the programs is only half of the problem.

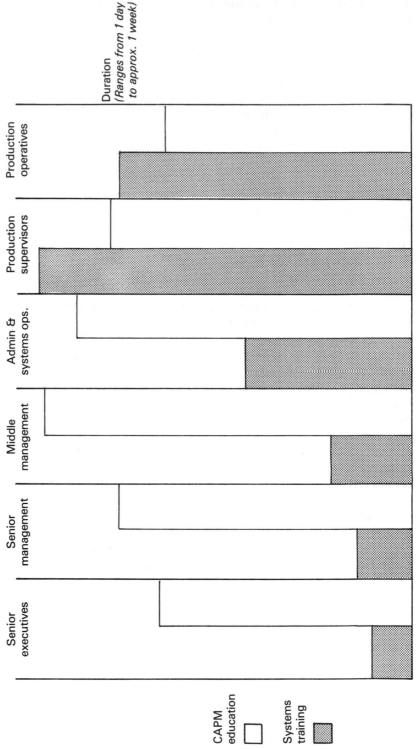

Duration
(Ranges from 1 day
to approx. 1 week)

Production
operatives

Production
supervisors

Admin &
systems ops.

Middle
management

Senior
management

Senior
executives

CAPM
education

Systems
training

CAPM education requirements for each function

Group	Education	Timing
Executive officers	Corporate overview CAPM principles	early in project
Senior management	Corporate and operational overview CAPM principles	early in project
Middle management	CAPM principles and practice	after 'go' decision
Systems administration and operators	CAPM principles and practice	after 'go' decision
Production supervisor	CAPM overview and departmental operations	after selection of system
Production operatives	CAPM overview and departmental operations	before going live

If the average implementation project is any indication, as well as educating people in the theory and practice of CAPM there might well be a need for some basic manufacturing management education. Even with people in positions such as inventory or production controller, it is surprising how poor their knowledge can be about the subjects at which they make their living. The systems which they operate may never have called upon them to know or understand first principles and they may well have learned their jobs from others who also had little of this knowledge.

This is often why systems fail to run an organization efficiently, why companies encounter major difficulties, and why they remain a very poor investment or go out of business altogether – lack of knowledge. In short, many people in key positions don't really know what they are doing. They are simply following a set of rules: if A happens, do X; if B happens, do Y. As a result they may run a bad system very well, but it will still be a bad system. You can call it 'back to basics' or "never mind the high tech, get the low tech right". It simply means that the operation of a CAPM system should be based on the same things as any good business should – a thorough knowledge of the principles on which it operates. Implementing a CAPM system will do nothing to resolve production or material problems if those problems have arisen because of ignorance. All that will happen is that one badly-run system will be replaced by another.

Systems training needs

At an early stage, probably just after the decision has been taken to implement a CAPM system, a training needs analysis should be carried out by a qualified person. The object here is to discover the strengths and weaknesses in the knowledge of those who will be coming into direct contact with the new systems, or indeed anyone who has to practice the various disciplines required to run a production unit efficiently. This is not to discover who needs training in the new systems – every user will need that – but to be able to provide the training which will bring everyone up to scratch on the principles which underlie them, such as stock control, production control, purchasing and shopfloor data collection. Once these needs have been assessed, the most appropriate way of fulfilling them is either in-house or external courses can be arranged.

Training

Training those who are to operate the system is absolutely essential for its smooth and efficient running and to ensure that the full return on investment is gained. Like education, this type of training tends to be expensive, but it should not be foregone or skimped on the grounds that the software is 'user friendly' and the operators will soon find their way around it with the aid of the user's manual. Apart from the fact that user manuals can range from the perfect to the useless, what (costly) mistakes are going to be made or opportunities missed while operators blunder around trying to teach themselves? One company which installed a CAPM system containing an MRP module, and which could have saved considerable time and effort by using it, still did not have MRP operational three years after its implementation because the material controller had never been taught how to operate it, the user manual could not enlighten him and the vendor either did not know or did not care.

All of those who are to regularly operate the various parts of the system must be thoroughly trained in their use of it, including those who will take over in the event of absence. The training courses must be specific to the programs purchased, and this implies that they will be carried out by the systems vendor, although this work is sometimes sub-contracted. The quality of user training provided should have been one of the criteria on which package selection was based, so that you can, with confidence, engage the vendor to carry it out. The vendor should suggest a sequence for the implementation of the various software programs, taking into account your own preferences. In any event, the training program will largely be determined by the installation schedule and must be timed to give the maximum benefit. Training on a specific subject carried out too far ahead of the implementation date for that program will be half-forgotten by the time the date comes around; too late, and time will have been wasted during the preparation stages. User training does not have to take place before any preparation work is carried out prior to implementation. The gathering and checking of data, for example in BOM and product routings, can commence as soon as the decision has been taken to implement a CAPM system. However, the training should have been carried out by the time the data is ready for entry into the system; that is, gathered, checked and in the correct format.

Like the education sessions, the training can either take place in-house or externally. Whichever one is chosen will depend, among other things, on the number of people to be trained, the computer hardware required to run the training programs and the facilities available within the company. How distant the training venue is from the manufacturing site might also be important, with preference being for the work to be carried out at the vendor's premises where full hardware and software facilities should be available. It makes sense to check on this at the time of the systems demonstration, prior to the final systems selection being made. The training (as well as the earlier demonstration if possible) should be carried out on the same type of hardware as that which has been purchased, because learning about hardware operation is as much a part of the training process as is becoming familiar with systems principles and practices.

Using your company's data

Insofar as is practicable, training should be centred round the methods of your own company and should make use of real manufacturing data from it. In this way the learning process can be speeded up and practical answers to real problems given by the instructors. Demonstrations and exercises to teach people how to carry out MRP for bicycle manufacture is of limited usefulness if your company builds electronic control equipment with BOM running to dozens of pages. However, there may be good reasons why this is not feasible. To set up files of data extensive enough to give meaningful examples and exercises might take considerable time. This would not be within the scope of a normal training course, (which might be attended by others from a variety of organizations) and would have to be set up specially by the instructors, who would certainly wish to charge extra for it.

Instruction in the use of the CAPM systems can be made yet more relevant to your company's daily operations if those conducting the training have visited your manufacturing plant to gain a good understanding of operating methods and terminology. Valuable time can be lost in a training session while pupils and teacher struggle to understand each others' different usage of the same terms, eg a contract, a job, a works order. Like all forms of training, this should be made as relevant as possible to the day-to-day working of the department or section by which it will be used. Many people are naturally resistant to change, especially that which might affect them directly and profoundly, and any steps that can be taken to mitigate its impact, by showing familiar elements alongside the new ones, should be considered.

There will be apprehensiveness on the part of some trainees because they have never laid a finger on a keyboard before, because they have not been in a formal learning situation since leaving school many years before, or simply because they feel that the training is also intended to be a surreptitious test of their abilities and that individual performances will be reported to their managers. These fears must be assuaged. Some individuals will emerge during training as being more adept than others at acquiring certain computer or systems skills and techniques. The rate of learning differs from one person to another and from one subject to another. The slow ones should be given extra time and assistance. They might need a place apart, with keyboard and screen, where they can sit and make their mistakes in private until they can build up enough self-confidence to come back into the main sessions once more. The training of operators in a CAPM system is not about conducting a course in a rigid format and at a predetermined pace, regardless of the abilities of the participants. It is to do with teaching each person how to get the best out of the systems and from him or herself, for the benefit of both the company and the individual.

CAPM training requirements

Group	Training	Timing
Systems administration	Detailed systems training	After system selection
System operators	Detailed program training	After system delivery
Production supervisor	Systems appreciation and selective training	After system delivery
Production workers	Systems appreciation and selective training	Immediately prior to going live

It will not be possible or indeed necessary for all of those requiring training to attend off-site courses given by the systems vendor's training department. This should be reserved for those whose main function it will be to run the system, such as inventory controllers, production controllers and purchasing officers. Many others will come into direct contact with the system, by receiving documentation from it, entering data or making enquiries at a terminal. This latter group will require an indication of the system's corporate dimension and a good appreciation of how it will work in their departments. The training they receive will be relatively narrow in scope, focusing purely on those parts of the system, a combination of manual and computerized, in which they will be directly involved.

There are two reasons why this training for shopfloor personnel should not be carried out by the systems vendor. Firstly, these courses are normally structured around individual system modules or programs, while the requirement here may only be for selected parts of some modules. Secondly, those using the system on the shopfloor (ie production foremen and operatives) need to be presented with a system which integrates the manual aspects with the computerized ones, and this cannot be done by the vendor. Those who do attend the vendor's training courses should therefore set up departmental instruction sessions for shopfloor personnel, in order to pass on the appropriate parts of what they have learned. This will not only ensure that the training is relevant and not generalized for everyone regardless of function, but will also reinforce the knowledge of the instructors, who may be either the systems administrators or operators instructing the production supervisors, or each supervisor instructing his or her work group.

Finally, it must be borne in mind that while the bulk of each person's training will be in those parts of the system with which he or she will be most closely involved, everyone must have some instruction, or at least a good appreciation of, any other systems which interface with these. For example, a purchasing officer may have no direct responsibility for inventory control or MRP, yet should be conversant with the way in which those systems operate and how they affect his or her function. To ensure that everyone is given instruction in those systems which are important for the proper execution of their duties, a training plan should be drawn up, an example of which is given below.

Training plan

Job Title	Primary	Secondary
Purchasing officer	Purchase order Processor	Inventory control
		MRP
Sales processors	Sales order processing	Sales forecasting MPS Inventory control Production scheduling

Job Title	Primary	Secondary
Process planner	Process planning	BOM Production routeing
Production supervisors	Work-in-process	Capacity planning
	Shop documentation	Shop scheduling Works ordering
Inventory controller	Inventory control	MRP Purchasing order processing Sales order processing
Production controller	Capacity planning Shop scheduling Work-in-process	Production routeing MPS Works ordering

CHAPTER 10

Laying the Foundations

Among other things, in the preceding chapters we have examined how a company might set about acquiring a CAPM system and preparing for its implementation. Firstly there should be a business plan, within which context the feasibility study will take place. Then a systems specification needs to be drawn up, potential systems vendors chosen and invited to tender for the hardware and software. An implementation plan is necessary so that the many elements of the chosen systems can be scheduled and co-ordinated efficiently, ensuring a smooth implementation in each section of the manufacturing organization.

All of these actions are necessary, but there is more that remains to be done. The systems you have acquired and are about to implement may be right for your organization, but is your organization right for the systems? Are all job functions going to be the same after implementation as they were before? Are those parts of the present systems which will remain, capable of bonding seamlessly with the new ones? Such questions must be answered before the implementation proper can proceed, and where possible should have been resolved early in the life of the project. Not only will this ensure a smooth transition from one set of systems to another, it will also assure the manufacturing personnel that any possible adverse effects of the systems implementation on their jobs have been considered and plans laid to mitigate them. The workforce is by far the most important asset which any manufacturing company has, and it is no more than common sense and good management to take it into the confidence of management as far as is commercially possible.

There are therefore three key elements which should be addressed in order that conditions can be conducive to good implementation; these are organization structure, job functions and manual systems. The organization structure supports the whole manufacturing enterprise and defines relationships between various job functions, which

113

in their turn make the business operate by the use of systems. Simply because these were adequate under previous methods of working does not mean that they are acceptable for a CAPM system. Indeed if a radical solution is chosen, such as a change from conventional Western methods of manufacturing to those of the JIT philosophy, there will almost certainly have to be major upheavals in all three of these areas. This will be less so where the introduction of either a full or part CAPM system is in fact the computerization of existing manual systems or the replacement of earlier computerized ones, yet in every instance, these aspects should be examined by an experienced and critical eye to ensure that the foundations for CAPM are appropriate.

Organization stucture

In the same way as systems can grow unheeded over the years, in an attempt to respond to the needs of a business an organization structure can grow in all directions until it bears little resemblance to the form in which it started. Because of its organic nature it expands and replicates parts of itself, but unlike natural organisms which normally do this in a logical and controlled manner, the corporate variety is often built up by a series of isolated steps which have been taken for the sake of expediency and are not always designed with the whole organization structure in mind. Alternatively, the structure may be of a form most appropriate to conditions and methods of working which will no longer obtain under CAPM. Functions which were previously essential may change their nature and begin to diminish, to merge with other like functions or disappear. What was the responsibility of one section or department may become that of another, until the character of the organization has changed significantly.

In manufacturing companies, as much as in other areas of business, the organization structure and its importance are often neglected and undervalued. How many executives have to hand an up-to-date version of their organization and an accurate idea of when it was last reviewed or restructured? What logic if any governed its initial structuring and how relevant is that to present day conditions? Many such structures have never been designed or examined by anyone with expertise in this subject, and it is therefore reasonable to assume that a significant number of them are ill-fitted for the uses to which they are put. It is in such instances that one finds the sales director who, for historical reasons, has responsibility for part of the production function, or the Purchasing Department reporting to the chief accountant. People get comfortable with known relationships and are loathe to change, even though the circumstances in which they operate may have altered substantially. And in the same way as happens with systems, the people who operate them can come to function quite well within a poorly-structured organization, although it is merely making the best of a bad job.

Is there any one type of organization which is most appropriate for a manufacturing company using CAPM systems? No, because it will also depend on the nature of the business and its size. What can be said is that any method of examining, and if necessary restructuring, the 'family tree' must be logical and comprehensive, and should initially at least take no account of the skills or lack of them of the present incumbents. Most of these type of hierarchical structures tend to be seen, as indeed they are drawn, as a pyramid, with the chief executive at the apex and a broad band of operatives forming the base. In evaluating organizational requirements for CAPM (or for any other purposes) advantage can often be gained by viewing the pyramid inverted; that is, from the broadest part downwards, so that basic organizational requirements on the shopfloor create a demand at the next level down, and so on to the chief executive officer at the bottom of the structure, in a kind of ripple effect. Having broadly or crudely determined the structure of the organization in this way, it would then be necessary to carry out a rationalization from the top down in the normal manner, so that any new format is tempered by convention and practicality.

Changes imposed by CAPM

The changes imposed by CAPM on an organization structure can be many and various. On the one hand it may mean the creation of a new post, such as that of master production scheduler, to facilitate the running of an MRP system. On the other hand, it could involve something more radical, as in the company which merged two departments, estimating and process planning because each estimate that they drew up needed to be so comprehensive that it virtually constituted a process plan. As every process plan (and BOM) required was already on file as an estimate, albeit in a more crude form, the job of drawing up each plan was more one of adapting existing data rather than creating new data. Of course this had also been the case in the previous manual systems, but it took the critical examination of the status quo which should accompany all CAPM implementation to make this clear. In extreme cases, where the organization has had an informal structure with ill-defined functions, where everyone 'pitches in' (recommended by some for flexibility and egalitarianism), CAPM will impose such discipline that the organization will require radical change. However, as the majority of manufacturing in the jobbing, batch or continuous process companies will take place under conventional structures, there should be little need for major reorganization. There may be a reduction in clerical input as time-consuming manual tasks are computerized; previous tasks may cease and be replaced by new and similar ones, such as the creation of MPS in place of the old production programs. In extreme cases a whole section within the company may disappear, for example where a computerized incentive scheme automatically carries out the required calculations from wage rates and shopfloor performance data on file, thereby obviating the need for bonus clerks.

It is important that the implications of the CAPM system implementation on all the personnel are determined as early as possible in the project. Once these have become clear, a policy should be formulated to deal with those situations which arise, such as jobs being made wholly or partly redundant or people being asked to take on different responsibilities. Too often, companies neglect this aspect of the project and do nothing about it until the last moment, creating resentment and ill-feeling among their employees. Where widespread computerization is about to take place in an organization, it is natural for people to fear that some jobs will be replaced by machines, and as is usual in such cases, the vacuum created by ignorance of the facts will be filled by rumour and speculation. If management show that they are aware of such potential problems and have given time and effort to their resolution, they will be much more likely to have the support of the workforce which is vital to a successful implementation. In any event, the implementation of a CAPM system rarely seems to require any major pruning of staff, and for this reason the potential savings in wages and salaries should rarely be used as a financial justification for the project. It is much more likely that people freed from one job will be required in another position, perhaps to assist in the preparation and interpretation of valuable information which could never have been available under the former manual system.

The advent of an integrated CAPM system in a company, whether it replaces a manual one or one which is part-computerized and part-manual, will have far-reaching and long-term effects on many parts of the organization. The structure of that organization need not be radically different simply to accommodate CAPM. After all, the system should have been chosen to fit your company's philosophy and methods of working, rather than your company being adapted to fit the system. Nevertheless, some change may be necessary, and it is important that these are decided by the steering committee as early as possible and recommendations made to the senior executives.

Job functions and how they are affected

Although in most cases CAPM may have little effect on the organization structure, if it is replacing less sophisticated, manual systems, there will be a considerable effect on many of the key jobs such as inventory controller, production controller and purchasing officer. Data which took time and effort to gather and process can be handled much more quickly, can be analysed more thoroughly and will be able to be transferred automatically to other parts of the system and used to give information and to create yet more data. Many parts of the system will now be accessible to all systems users by computer, providing data which would otherwise be unavailable at an acceptable cost, if at all. This does not mean that systems users will become so efficient that their work will be completed by lunch-time, but rather that much of the drudgery will be taken away from their work and they will be able to accomplish things which would have been impossible under the old system.

As might be expected, there may be a down-side to all of this. When individuals run systems for their own use or that of a small group the systems may be configured in such a way as to be readily understandable only by the users, perhaps by the use of some kind of shorthand or symbolism. In an integrated CAPM system, one of the major strengths is the ability to pass data from one sub-system to another and have it understood by those who do not have specific knowledge of disciplines other than their own. This immediately requires that most if not all data has a corporate dimension. The salesman at a computer terminal in his office can enquire as to the production program for the weeks ahead; does he understand the figures given and have some appreciation of how they were calculated? The production planner may wish to look at the purchasing records to check future raw material availability; does the purchasing officer order some materials by weight while the inventory records are by linear measurement? These may seem trivial considerations, but it is vital that all of the sub-systems are rationalized and clearly understood, even by casual users, if costly mistakes are to be avoided.

Assuming that a manufacturing company is moving from largely manual systems to one integrated CAPM system, what are the main changes to be expected and their likely effects on the job functions of key systems users? These will vary from company to company, dependent on the nature and volume of business and the way in which it is conducted. Care should be taken prior to the implementation, in determining the effects of the new systems on individual job functions, some examples of which are given below.

Sales Order Processing (SOP)

The introduction of a SOP system can have a minimal effect on the sales function and simply be a computerization of the manual procedures. This would tend to be the case in a company where products are made-to-order and the system is merely used to record order details prior to manufacture and recall them for invoicing purposes after the goods have been produced and despatched. At the other extreme, where products are sold from stock, a computerized SOP system can make a significant difference to the way in which the task of processing is carried out. This may require an increase in the calibre of people who carry out sales order processing, although in the case of telephone sales, it may reduce the number of people required to do it. Under the manual system, sales orders might well have been taken for products regardless of current stocks or future capacity to produce them, followed later by checks against stock records and production schedules, possibly ending with a call back to the customer to change the initial delivery estimate. With an integrated system available for this type of order-taking, direct access can be had to current inventory data, for both 'in stock' and 'on order' quantities, giving the customer a more immediate and definite response and the ability to make decisions based on factual information. This makes for a more dynamic situation for those processing sales orders, which may call for an increased level of interaction with customers and skills which were not required by the previous methods of working.

Inventory control

As a sub-system which is central to the main CAPM system, many of the changes will come from the ability to exchange data automatically with other sub-systems such as SOP (for finished goods), purchasing (for raw materials) and possibly MRP. Instead of spending most of his or her time updating stock records, and a minimum of it regulating re-order levels and quantities, determining batch sizes and so forth, the inventory controller can manage inventory more efficiently and improve response to demand by concentrating on the latter activities. He or she may no longer be in sole control of inventory records, as the SOP program automatically allocates stock to sales orders and downdates stock records when an order is despatched. If the new systems contain an MRP module, the inventory controller may be able to take on the running of it, due to the time saved in purely inventory control duties. All of this may call for a different range of skills than previously required (especially if MRP is involved) as the job decreases its clerical content and expands into work which is more dynamic and driven by decision-making.

Purchasing

Again, much of this function under a manual system can be taken up by tedious clerical work: raising purchase orders; entering them onto the stock records or passing them to inventory control for this to be done; keeping track of what has been booked and what has not; and monitoring the status of each purchase order to determine its due date, quantity delivered and quantity outstanding. With the advent of CAPM, much of this should be done by the system: order quantities automatically posted to the 'on order' columns of the inventory records, the entering of goods received data updating the purchasing and inventory programs. Tracking of orders and reminders of due dates can be carried out by the purchasing program, while various configurations of material cost price can be calculated automatically and vendor analyses performed. Such facilities would generally have the effect of producing a greater breadth and quality of information more quickly than a manual system could, thereby saving the purchasing officer time which could be devoted to his or her primary task, the evaluation and selection of the optimum products for the company's requirements. In allowing this individual to become more involved in the actual purchasing aspect of the job, instead of merely acting as a clerk, better buying decisions can be made and the unit cost of many materials reduced.

Production control

In CAPM terms this can cover a number of different areas, namely capacity planning, works ordering, shopfloor scheduling and work-in-progress, and as such will have an effect on a variety of job functions. The first and most obvious ones will be those of the production control staff who will now have at their disposal a powerful means of calculating and recalculating all of the various options which arise in attempting to match available production capacity to the ever-changing demands placed upon it. Many manual systems are operated with approximate figures (often euphemistically termed 'flexibility'), with a block or 'bucket' of time being allocated to each operation which has to be performed, even though there may be considerable differences in the actual times taken. Individual jobs are loosely scheduled, with shopfloor supervisors being left to their own devices when it comes to placing jobs at the various work centres. Monitoring work-in-process, through a complex production plant using manual methods, is extremely difficult to do without a high degree of supervision and clerical work. In these circumstances, often the only degree to which tracking is carried out on individual batches is the recording of a finished job or a physical search by a progress chaser on the shopfloor if the stage of manufacture of a particular batch has to be determined. The production control element of CAPM suddenly imposes the need for much greater detail, and in turn provides a wealth of detail with which to make decisions. Being itself capable of great precision, the computer system will require more precision and discipline from its users than many manual systems, if the best use is to be made of it. This may well mean a change in the nature of job functions in production control, both in planning and shopfloor control, with a

119

greater degree of sophistication being introduced and the accent moving away from 'firefighting' to planning and monitoring.

Analysis of present systems

Before the new CAPM systems are implemented, it will be necessary to scrutinize those parts of the present systems, whether manual or computerized, which will need to be retained and interfaced with the new ones. As has been stated in an earlier chapter, this is not the job of the CAPM system vendor, but must fall to the consultant or to the project leader. There is a kind of demarcation line around any computer system, the points at which reports are requested and produced, where data is entered or information is given on screen. Anything outside of this the computer system does not treat. Decisions have to be made, such as when the various reports are to be requested and by whom, who enters data, from where is it obtained and what courses of action are open to the operator, based on information given on screen. All of this and more will have to be decided and laid down in some kind of procedures manual.

It is likely that there will already be procedures in existence to cater for those parts of your manufacturing systems which are not to be computerized, for example the gathering of shopfloor data, or the periodic review of raw materials inventory parameters. If not, then they will have to be devised and put in place at the same time as the CAPM systems. A thorough review should be carried out of all such procedures in each department, to ensure that they are compatible with the new systems in every respect. In many instances it will be found that the new CAPM systems do not fit well with existing company systems, primarily because the new systems offer features and capabilities which the old ones never could execute, eg, perpetual inventory listings, stock movement reports, detailed job costings. Tasks which previously needed to be done manually will now be carried out by computer, data which was notified by one department to another by the passage of documentation will now be accomplished by viewing a computer screen; reports will have to be scrutinized and acted upon, the status of various orders monitored and procedures such as MRP set in motion at the appropriate time.

Every company will be different, so it is difficult to give detailed instructions as to how to proceed in each sub-system, but some general guidelines are given below regarding those areas which commonly need attention. In accordance with the model in Chapter One ('The Elements of CAPM'), these are given for each of the four main areas of project activity, namely forecasting, planning, execution and reporting.

Forecasting

It is not uncommon for a commercial enterprise, even a fairly substantial one, to operate without the benefit of a business plan, and manufacturing companies are no exception. While an integrated computer system does not require a business plan in order to operate effectively, the context in which the system is run and the underlying assumptions should certainly be provided by such a plan. It is similar to a sales forecast in that it attempts to predict future events, something which businessmen in general, and salesmen in particular, are usually reluctant to do. A business plan should be drawn up once a year and a detailed sales forecast compiled at more frequent intervals. There is little point in sales personnel saying that this cannot be done, since it is upon such a forecast that personnel, money and machines will be committed in production, and if a plan is not forthcoming from the Sales Department then it will have to be devised by production, who do not have the necessary market knowledge and cannot plan in an information vacuum. This production plan, or Master Production Schedule (MPS), must be detailed enough in terms of product quantities and timings to allow some broad comparisons to be made between planned output and production capacity, to ensure that the MPS is realistic. These are the main elements of the forecasting phase in most CAPM systems. In one form or another they are often present in manual or partly-computerized systems, but not normally to the same level of detail or accuracy. Therefore it will probably be necessary to set up procedures involving the sales, marketing, inventory and production functions which will gather the necessary data, discuss and agree it and then present it in a format suitable for entry into the appropriate computer programs. This may be a radical step for those manufacturing companies which previously ran three different businesses, those being a sales business, an inventory business and a production business, but it is a necessary step and has the added advantage of forcing all concerned to think corporately instead of merely departmentally.

Planning

In this phase of CAPM systems operation, with an achievable production plan determined, the detailed work of material control and capacity planning takes place. In order to achieve this, systems must be in place which will provide the accurate data required, and this area usually gives most cause for concern because the accuracy of data for inventory control, BOM, work centres and product routings in manual systems is so often much lower than that demanded by computerized systems. People who work with this inaccurate data know of its shortcomings and make mental allowances as they use it.

121

Thus a BOM which calls for one type of material, now discontinued, will automatically have another type substituted because everyone knows of the change, although the bill has not been altered since no-one has been made responsible for doing so and there are no procedures laid down. Let us look at each of these four areas in turn, to see what aspects of the present systems might have to be altered in order to conform to the new systems.

Inventory control

It is not enough that an appropriate computer system is used for the recording of inventory transactions and status. Those manual methods used to gather inventory data must also be efficient and capable of the required accuracy. Procedures and documentation relating to inventory must be scrutinized, including:

- Goods inwards – goods received notes (GRNs), material certification procedures, quality checks and rejections.
- Placing materials into stock, the location and traceability system.
- Physical stockchecking procedures, inventory security, for both raw materials and finished goods.
- Stock issuing procedures, material requisitions, kitting lists and methods, floor stocks, returns to stock.
- The recording of finished goods production, including scrap, the location system.
- Finished goods picking, despatch methods and documentation.

Bills of Material (BOM)

- The creation of bills at the design stage or later.
- Procedures for making changes to bills.
- Maintenance of costs on bills.

Work centres

- Maintenance of data on machine and labour capacities.
- Machine and labour efficiency data.
- Maintenance of work centre costs.

Product routeings

- Maintenance of routeing data.
- Engineering change control.
- Process planning methods and documentation.

Execution

The execution phase of a CAPM system is mainly comprised of three areas, ie the raising of works and purchase orders, the scheduling of work through the production departments and the monitoring of work-in-process. This phase and the following one, reporting, are usually less reliant on manual systems interfaces than the first two. If an MRP module is being used, then suggested works and purchase orders will be an automatic output, and there are systems available which raise the required orders without further human intervention. In such cases, the system is completely contained in the computer software. On the other hand, while the calculations for shop scheduling are carried out by the computer, the system of determining priorities beforehand and conveying work-to list data to the shopfloor afterwards, is a manual activity and must be compatible with the computer ones.

Increasingly, manufacturing companies are turning to electronic means of shopfloor data capture such as bar-code readers, in order to reduce costs and increase speed and accuracy, yet there are considerable limitations on the applicability of these techniques, and there will always remain a large number of companies in which manual methods of monitoring work-in-process will remain dominant. In terms of data gathering, this is one of the most important areas of manufacturing management. It is here that the progress of individual works orders is determined, and data is fed back to the shop scheduling program for updating and for rescheduling to take place if necessary. Manual systems for recording production and scrap quantities, labour and lost time must be checked for effectiveness, so that the CAPM programs can work effectively. One of the commonest causes of poor results from CAPM systems is not the shortcomings of the software itself but the inaccurate data fed to it from the shopfloor.

Reporting

Financial and operational feedback are the two elements which make up the last of the four phases, and those which are the most automatic of all in an integrated CAPM system. In such an instance, for example, vendor invoice data will be passed both to the purchasing and accounts payable programs, sales data to the accounts receivable program and manufacturing costs to the job, product or contract costing module. On the Operational front, production levels and machine and labour efficiencies will be calculated as a matter of course.

All of this is to little avail if procedures are not in place which ensure that three actions are regularly taken:
1. Appropriate reports are printed, detailing financial and operational performance.
2. These reports are scrutinized by responsible people.
3. Remedial action is taken on any deficiencies found.

CHAPTER 11

Making the Change

The successful implementation of a CAPM system in a manufacturing company depends on one thing above all others – good planning and control. In Chapter Eight we examined in some detail the use of an Implementation Plan to determine what should be done, the timing and the resources required. In this chapter we will consider firstly the role of those drawing up the plan, the steering committee and the project leader, the other tasks which they must perform, and the implementation of the applications software into the various company functions. In addition, the effect of the new systems on the organization's workforce, its customers and its suppliers will be considered.

The steering committee

The steering committee should be set up at the earliest possible date in the life of the project, so that it can oversee all aspects of it and make regular reports to the chief executive officer and senior executives. As we shall see, the project leader will decide upon which tactics are to be employed and will act as the day-to-day manager of the selection and implementation process, while the steering committee (of which the project manager is a member) will consider the broader issues and determine the strategy. There are a number of useful guidelines when forming a steering committee for CAPM implementation:

- It should be of a reasonable size, consisting of no fewer than four persons and ideally no more than eight. If it gets much larger than eight, the number of potential interactions and conflicts between the members multiplies alarmingly and the possibility of accomplishing useful work and reaching decisions diminishes at an equally rapid rate.

- The committee should represent the main functional areas within the organization eg sales/marketing, design, process planning, production, production control, buying, inventory control, finance. Just about everyone will want to become a member, as they will believe that their views will not be properly represented if they do not, but this should be resisted at all costs and each department assured that their views will be canvassed and considered.
- With the exception of the committee chairman, who may be a senior executive, it is usually preferable if the members are comprised of people at a similar management level to each other, ideally middle management. The committee should not be made up of senior executives or a mixture of management levels, as the more senior ones tend to dominate meetings and the others defer to them. Besides, the people on the committee should bc those with direct and detailed knowledge of the various manufacturing methods and systems in operation, and these would normally be middle managers.
- It should be made clear to all potential committee members, that is, before they accept the positions, that the necessary time will be allowed for them to carry out the requisite work, and that the committee will be held jointly responsible for successful implementation. They must also be aware, when a representative is requested from a department or section, that what is required is a knowledgeable person with the authority to make decisions in committee, and not a departmental junior who is seconded to the committee because the senior people are uninterested.

Having overseen the project from the beginning – taking it through the various stages from initial interest to systems selection – the steering committee must now be prepared to devote a considerable amount of time and energy to the job of implementation. In this context, the main duties of the committee are:

1. Deciding the policies and constraints within which the implementation will take place, eg that the next phase of implementation will not take place until the previous one is running effectively.
2. Deciding the sequence in which the various CAPM software modules will be installed.
3. Choosing personnel to take part in the task forces which are set up.
4. Determining what resources will be required and ensuring that these are made available.
5. Giving guidance to the project manager and supporting him or her when required.
6. Monitoring the progress of the project and making decisions on rescheduling of significant aspects of the project. The day-to-day or

tactical matters should be left to the judgement of the project manager.

As well as ensuring that the membership of the committee is composed of representative and sufficiently senior personnel, it should be made clear by the chairman that meetings should be regularly attended. If the member cannot attend, and this should only be allowed *in extremis,* a well-briefed deputy should be appointed and given decision-making authority. Minuted meetings should be held regularly, preferably once a fortnight, and an agenda followed. It is all too easy for such discussions to degenerate into lengthy arguments about the minutiae of procedures and documentation, or to dispute what was said at previous meetings, while the main decisions remain unmade. Personal animosities and old rivalries between departments can easily arise if the meetings are inadequately controlled, especially when the project runs into trouble during implementation.

Most likely in the medium-sized company, and certainly in the small ones that are implementing CAPM systems, those who are members of the steering committee will also be task group leaders, charged with carrying out specific activities, either personally or with the assistance of their departmental staff; for example, checking the completeness and accuracy of BOM data or applying a new coding and classification system to piece parts and raw materials. On the one hand, such an arrangement has the advantage that the task group leaders are fully aware of all aspects of the project through their presence on the committee. On the other hand, it means a considerable extra workload for people who must already be fully occupied running the business. It must be realized from the start that this is an inevitable part of implementing a CAPM system. Certain work, like the initial entry of data into the computer files, can be done by temporary labour, in this instance keyboard operators hired for the task, but the main burden will have to be borne by company personnel with the delegation of some normal duties where possible. It will rapidly become clear that, whereas most people will be happy to have the benefits which the new systems will bring, their willingness to take on a considerable extra workload will be quite another matter. The maintenance of motivation will be particularly crucial in the early stages of the project, where it will be all work and no benefits, and the key person at that time, and indeed throughout the whole exercise, will be the project manager.

The project manager

Just as it is essential to have a body of knowledgeable people in the form of a committee to determine the policies governing the project

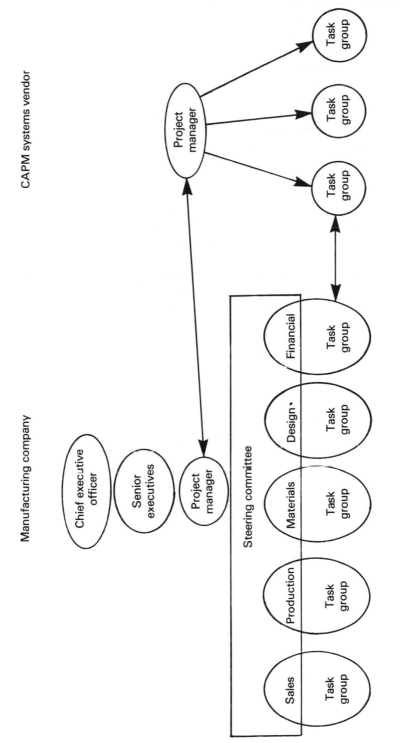

Figure 11.1 *CAPM project organization*

and the supervision of it, there is also a requirement for someone to undertake the day-to-day management of it. This is the role of the project manager, the single most important person involved in the implementation, and it is vital that the appointee should be chosen with considerable care. He or she may be someone from within the company seconded to the job, or brought in from outside, possibly with a view to staying on as systems administrator when the implementation is complete. If your company is part of a group, there may be assistance available from central services or from someone who has been a project manager for a CAPM system project in a sister company.

One common mistake made by manufacturing organizations implementing CAPM systems is to expect the consultant who has been engaged to take on the role of project manager. Unless the company is willing to pay large amounts of money to have the consultant in almost continuous attendance, an arrangement such as this will simply not work. The workload will naturally depend on the size of the company and the extent to which the systems are to be implemented, but in almost every case there will need to be an 'expert' on hand to answer queries and give assistance when difficulties are encountered, and this is very much the role of the project manager. In a large company, implementing a full CAPM system over a period of 18 months or less, the project manager's job is likely to be a full-time one. This will quickly become evident, and an appropriate person will then be appointed to the job. It is in the smaller company, where only a part-time project manager is required that the problems most frequently arise, due to the demands of both the CAPM duties and his or her normal job. Something has to give, and the only way for the problem to be resolved is for an assessment to be made of the time to be expended each week on the project and assistance given with the project manager's normal duties for a comparable period of time. Poor project management is almost a guarantee of failure for a CAPM systems implementation, and unfortunately it is often the case that in the conflict between the project manager's two loyalties, running the business and implementing CAPM, the computer project comes a long way behind. Of course, running the business must always be given top priority, but the computerization of systems must run it a close second.

In any event, the person chosen must have certain skills and knowledge if he or she is to stand any chance of seeing the project through to a successful conclusion:

- He or she must have a good knowledge of CAPM, if not in practice then certainly in principle, based on a sound knowledge of its underlying disciplines such as inventory control, capacity planning, and where appropriate the specific philosophy which is being adopted, such as MRP II, OPT or JIT.

- He or she must have, by virtue of their normal position in the company, or be given by senior management, sufficient authority over those who are to carry out the project work.
- Some experience of project planning and management is desirable, especially if extensive systems are to be implemented in a large organization.
- The person should be enthusiastic about the project and be able to communicate that enthusiasm to everyone involved. He or she must be a leader.
- He should have broad management experience in the manufacturing industry in general and preferably in the industry sector of the company which is to be computerized. In this way he or she will be aware of the differing demands and requirements of each section or department.

The project manager should take up the appointed role as soon as possible in the life of the project. The more involved he or she is in systems definition and selection, the more they should be committed to the chosen one and the greater will be their knowledge of the present and proposed systems, the manufacturing and administrative processes within your company and the people with whom they will work. The responsibilities and duties which he or she will be required to carry out following system selection should be drawn up in the form of a job specification and include such items as:

- Drawing up the implementation plan and managing the available resources in such a way as to achieve the target dates within it.
- Assessing the workload for the various tasks to be carried out, and advising on the formation and staffing of the task groups.
- Planning and supervising the education and training programme for systems users and others.
- Being the primary contact with the systems vendor, advising them of company decisions and ensuring that they adequately perform any actions required.
- Assisting in the preparation of project budgets and managing events within these financial constraints.
- Monitoring the progress of all aspects of the project, informing the committee at each meeting and submitting a short written report to senior executives each month.

If engaged, the role of the consultant in all of this can be at whatever level is decided by the company. Often he or she will assist in drawing up the implementation plan, appointing the steering committee and selecting the project manager. This would especially be the case in the smaller organization where the project manager does not have all of the required experience and what is known and understood has to be augmented by that of the consultant. Apart from this, the consultant will mainly be used in an advisory capacity, attending each of the steering committee meetings and looking in some detail at the progress being made and problems encountered. An experienced consultant, properly utilized by the company, can be worth many times the fee which he or she charges. After all, your company is not only buying x weeks of work from the consultant but also y years of experience.

Sequence of implementation

Those who wish to implement a CAPM system in their company do not always have the luxury of choosing precisely when the project is to commence. Often it is a case of getting it up and running 'as soon as possible' so that savings can be made at the earliest opportunity or poor systems replaced before they do further damage. For all the plans that are meticulously laid and the good intentions, start dates may be delayed, causing a clash with other major events in the organization. All of this notwithstanding, recognition should be given to the fact that the preparation for and commencement of such a system should be given the highest possible priority and the most favourable timing should be planned. Such events as partial or complete plant moves, holiday periods or any kind of serious disruption to normal working methods should be avoided. The implementation will need every chance to succeed and should not be jeopardized by lack of forethought.

Having decided when the systems should be implemented, you must then consider in which order they are to be implemented. Some part of this will already have been decided for you. Assuming that a complete and integrated suite of CAPM programs is to be installed, you will find that certain of these need others to be in place before they can in turn become operational. For example, MRP cannot operate unless it is fed with data from the inventory control, BOM and MPS programs, and detailed capacity planning is hardly practical without product routings. These considerations apart, the steering committee must decide in which order the various modules are to be tackled. They can of course be installed piecemeal – say BOM, followed by SOP and then Works Orders, and temporarily operated in a 'stand-alone' mode. There may be good reasons for doing this. More commonly, programs would be implemented in sub-sets, such as those dealing with material planning and control, or those applying to the production processes, where the greatest benefit can be derived most quickly from the individual programs and their partial integration.

Simultaneous implementation

Some companies have attempted to implement the whole of a CAPM system simultaneously, that is, every module of the system 'going live' on the same day. There have no doubt been some successes using this method. There have also been some spectacular failures, with one manufacturing site experiencing such chaos in many of its sub-systems that it had to cease all operations and shut down the plant for two weeks, with massive loss of revenue, not to mention face. There is some argument in favour of this method, in that different personnel resources are used to implement the various parts of the system, ie financial, inventory control, production control, sales, but it is too much of an 'all or nothing' approach to appeal to any but the most confident or foolhardy.

Often there will be major problems being caused by the current systems in one area of the business (which may have prompted consideration of CAPM in the first place) and this will dictate the initial program implementations. As long as it is consistent with the demands of the particular software purchased, then those parts chosen for the first phase should be the ones which will fulfil the greatest need. If there are no overriding priorities, then it can often be most beneficial to implement the Inventory Control (raw material and/or finished goods) module first, and for three good reasons:
1. There are often large savings to be made by improved inventory control and reduced stockholding.
2. Inventory control is the base module for the wider material control sub-set (MRP, purchasing, etc).
3. It is important to have an early implementation success and inventory control is usually one of the 'easier' programs to implement successfully.

The last of these reasons throws an interesting light on the whole CAPM project, bringing out the very important psychological aspect of it, which is often as important as the technical and operational ones. Whatever they may say, there will almost always be people within the company who regard the whole thing with a jaundiced eye. It has been tried before and it did not work that time, either in this company or a previous one; the present systems work perfectly well and it is a waste of money to change them. Often these can be quite senior people in the organization and their opinions, if allowed wide currency, can mean death to any hopes of a good implementation. The enthusiasm of everyone connected with the project is required and in some instances this is hard earned. The best way of ensuring this is to have an early and demonstrable success. If not, the "I knew it would go wrong" attitude quickly emerges, support for the next phase wanes and because of this it is even less successful, and the whole project goes into an irrecoverable downward spiral. It cannot be stressed too frequently that the implementation of a CAPM system is difficult and often frustrating work. Every ounce of enthusiasm and support available within the organization is needed for success.

Dual processing

Another important topic which needs to be discussed at an early stage is that of dual processing; that is, whether any or all of the new system programs will be run simultaneously with the old systems for a trial period. There is no hard and fast rule here. It must be remembered that dual processing will almost certainly mean a heavy increase in the workload for some people, especially at the beginning when they will be unfamiliar with the new systems and will tend to double-check everything that they do. Whether or not dual processing is carried out may depend on a number of factors, for example:

● If there is currently another computer system in use, and the new system requires different hardware, is there sufficient space to accommodate two sets of hardware – screens, keyboards, printers and CPU – in accessible positions?
● Can the manual systems be set up to provide data in the two different formats that may be required, bearing in mind that this may mean such things as two sets of all documentation?
● Is sufficient manpower available to handle two systems without affecting manufacturing efficiency and the level of customer service?

If the answer to these questions is in the affirmative, then dual processing is likely to be supportable. It is certainly the 'belt-and-braces' way to implement a CAPM system, but there are considerable costs involved. Much of what will be done can only be a dummy run, because two systems with different philosophies and techniques are likely to produce different answers, and both recommended actions cannot be executed. For example, this would be the case where, under the present system, the shopfloor supervisors determined the job sequence at the work centres, whereas under the CAPM system this was determined by the shopfloor scheduling system.

One alternative to dual processing is to terminate the old system one day and start the new one the next day. This has the advantage of making a clean break with the old one and of saving considerable effort (and no small amount of confusion) on dual processing. It can of course be a 'make or break' situation, but at least this has the advantage of concentrating the minds of the participants on the need for success. The confidence of success displayed by those companies which go for the 'clean break' option will almost certainly be engendered by thorough preparation. The choice of implementation method will depend on the criticality and recoverability of each subsystem being computerized, but generally speaking, the larger organizations would tend to go for the dual processing option, while the smaller ones are more likely to try and get by without it. In either event, make sure that previous records are retained for a minimum of three months after the start-up date for the new system.

Running a pilot program

A good compromise between these two methods is to run a pilot program in some section of the organization which is as near as possible to being a microcosm of the subject of the whole computerization project. This could be one manufacturing department, chosen because of its relative simplicity of operation, or another for its complexity, with the reasoning that if the new system works there it will work anywhere. Alternatively, there may be a self-contained part of the business which would be ideal. Much of the resources marshalled for the whole implementation can be brought to bear on the pilot one, thereby increasing the chances of success and scoring a psychological bull's-eye before the main event.

The effect on vendors and customers

The successful implementation of a new CAPM system in a manufacturing company does not only give benefits in terms of greater efficiency and improved staff morale. If handled correctly, there should also be some reward to be gained by publicizing your efforts. As yours is a progressive and forward-looking organization, it is embracing new technology not only in order to improve its competitiveness, but also for the benefit of its vendors and customers, whether these benefits are direct, such as an electronic link with the systems of other companies, or indirect, with a general improvement in the operating efficiency of your company.

There are practical reasons for letting other organizations know that new systems are being or have been introduced into various parts of your company. The documentation which you will send to them may be changed, for example the purchase order that is sent to the vendor, the order acknowledgement or sales invoice which the customer will receive. You may require that certain data from a customer, such as an order/delivery schedule, be sent in a particular format, or have to check whether a vendor can accept order documentation in the format in which your new system prints it. In those companies with more sophisticated systems, there may be the possibility of exchanging data electronically. This electronic data interchange (EDI) is an increasingly common method of placing and receiving sales orders, transferring information such as BOM or product specifications, company representatives interrogating files for stock availability using portable terminals. Substantial amounts of time and expense can be saved by such methods and the possibility of their use, subject to suitable security measures, should certainly be explored. Your organization may already have come under pressure from a major customer to conform to some of their administrative methods. Given the awesome economic power of many large corporations, this trend can only continue and grow.

If your organization has the confidence and ability to successfully implement an integrated CAPM system, then every possible public relations advantage should be gained from it. Details of the systems operation and benefits could be given in your company brochures and sales literature alongside the usual photographs of production facilities and information on the company's technical abilities. Such an implementation is the sign of an innovative organization which is prepared to spend effort and resources on improving its operations. With the increasing emphasis on raising efficiency in manufacturing companies and the widespread acceptance and application of such philosophies as total quality management (TQM), the pressure for beneficial change can only increase.

CHAPTER 12

Maintaining the System

Systems maintenance

It is easy to fall into the trap of thinking that when the whole CAPM system is installed and all the programs integrated, it is all plain sailing from there on. Of course, the difficult implementational work of gathering data, setting up files, devising new manual systems to interface with the computerized ones will have been completed. What remains to be done on a regular basis is the maintenance of the systems, and in this, CAPM is no different from most administrative systems. This is an area of vital importance, the neglect of which will inevitably result in the whole system becoming unworkable and practically useless.

Computers cannot distinguish wrong or redundant data from that which is current and accurate in the way that a human being can. So, part of the task of implementing the systems should be the drawing up of procedures to ensure that all files are regularly updated with what might be called static data, eg parts master records, as opposed to those containing volatile data, such as a purchase order file which would be automatically updated by the various transactions which take place in that program or any other which has an interface with it. In essence, such tasks are no different than in a manual system. Someone has to do them, and it may well be that the same persons do the same tasks as before the advent of CAPM, except that in many pre-CAPM companies (and a significant number of post-CAPM ones as well) the tasks are poorly carried out, if at all. As we shall see in the next chapter, this is one of the prime reasons for CAPM systems failure. After all the investment, all the hard work, the recriminations and final triumph, major parts of the system eventually grind to a halt or need the crutch of an unofficial manual system because nobody believes the numbers that the machine churns out. Simply changing from manual to computer systems will not cure the bad habits of a

corporate life time. It must be realized that poor systems maintenance on a computerized system will give worse results than on a
manual system every time. It is therefore worth investing a little time
and effort to make sure that sound procedures are laid down before
the system is operational, that everyone knows his responsibilities
and that regular checks or systems audits are carried out to see that
they are maintained. There are numerous aspects of a CAPM system
which will need to be monitored for change. Let us look at some of
the main ones in terms of what has to be done and which persons in
the organization are likely to do it.

Administrative procedures

The two aspects of the manufacturing systems which need to be
considered are those of *data* and *procedures*. The procedures are
there to make sure that all administrative operations are carried out
correctly, but also to see that both the static and volatile data are
maintained at a high level of accuracy. Both procedures and data
must be substantially correct most of the time for the systems to
function properly, and there must be a method in place for ensuring
that they are correct. One way of doing this is to draw up a set of
procedures for each sub-system and incorporate them into a manual.
This could be carried out by the consultant, the project manager or
perhaps someone in the organization who has experience in this sort
of work, such as a work study or production engineer. This should be
a formal document, or set of documents, with each copy numbered,
and the whole maintained in the manner of a quality assurance
manual. Changes to procedures should be authorized by senior
management and the systems users informed of the changes and
instructed in the new methods where necessary. One person should
be given the responsibility of maintaining the manual of procedures
by writing new ones when necessary and issuing replacement sheets
to copy holders. In this way, and provided the procedures fit the
operational requirements and are regularly audited, the growth of
informal methods alongside the official ones can be avoided.

The procedures manual should treat the methods to be used in
some detail, although it should stop short of describing the methods
to be used to input or extract data from the CAPM system. That is the
role of the systems user manual. The objective of your company's
manual is to provide efficient administrative procedures for the
running of the production function, and it should contain details of
the following:

- all manual systems to be used in each department or section,
  where and how they interface with the CAPM systems
- the position of each person responsible for the various
  procedures
- the frequency and timing of each action

- the methods to be used in each instance
- the sources of all data and documentation, and their destinations.

Data entry

One significant difference between manual planning and control systems in manufacturing, and those based on CAPM, is that the person nominally in charge of a particular sub-system, for example inventory control, does not have control over all the data entering the system nor the facility to monitor it easily. Under a manual system, as all data entered into a department's files was capable of being checked before entry by staff from that department, a good level of data accuracy could be maintained. Into most sub-systems on computer will come data compiled by other departments, automatically transferred from their programs, for example from SOP into finished goods inventory control. This means that CAPM systems are run on the premise that a large percentage of the data handled is accurate, since the computer system cannot view it with any critical faculty. Data from one sub-system is passed to others, both within the manufacturing site and perhaps also to remote locations via a datacommunications link. If a significant amount of data is inaccurate it can spread throughout the system like a disease and affect numerous aspects of the business. One only has to think of an underpriced raw material which is used in the manufacture of a variety of products. The creation, distribution and use of such data is widespread, and although there must be clear accountability for each part of it, everyone in the organization must be made aware of his or her responsibilities in this respect and realize the effect each individual can have on the system by using low-integrity data. Some of the major data elements are:

Sales forecast. The information from which this is created should be gathered constantly by the Sales Department and maintained by manual methods, or on computer if a forecasting program is part of the system. It is the single most important set of figures, as all actions within the organization follow from it – the type of product, the rate of production, the resources required, the profit margins and so forth.

Sales orders. These too will be entered and maintained by the Sales Department, though more likely by sales administration personnel than those engaged in field sales. It is especially important that non-users of the system, in this case salesmen and women, are aware of the need for accuracy and clarity, as the computer will not recognize shorthand product descriptions or know what products Smith and Company usually have. Static data will primarily consist of product and customer files, including price and discount details which must be strictly maintained, especially in those systems designed automatically to apply to sales orders the prices and discounts on file.

Master production schedules (MPS) and rough-cut capacity planning. In the larger company, this function would be run by a master production scheduler, but in the smaller organizations the work would probably be carried out by someone within the material or production control function, from data provided by others.

Inventory control. The static data held in the inventory control program's part master files may be for raw materials or finished goods. In the case of raw materials, this would probably be maintained by the inventory controller, with data supplied by purchasing (bought-out materials) and design or manufacturing (bought-out materials and made-in components). Finished goods static data could be maintained by inventory control or by sales personnel from data supplied by design or manufacturing, with purchasing giving details of any products bought in purely for re-sale. The volatile data in the inventory control program is often subject to the most widespread sourcing and input of any CAPM program – from goods inwards, stores, production, sales and MRP. Quantities are added and subtracted without the knowledge of, or checking by, those responsible for stock movements, the inventory control staff. It is essential that all system users are fully versed in the correct procedures and aware of the need for complete accuracy.

Bills of material (BOM). All of the data within a BOM is static, and the responsibility for its maintenance would normally lie with the Drawing Office, the Design Department or inventory control. This includes details of materials, components, alternatives, and the cost of each item on the bill. Such data would be provided by purchasing (costs), from your own design section or those of your customers. A high degree of accuracy is especially important in those CAPM systems which use an MRP module.

Capacity planning and scheduling. Work centre details, consisting of labour and machine capacity supplied by production, are held within this program, the upkeep of which would normally be the responsibility of the production controller. Although this data is by nature static, that is it is not subject to change by interaction with other data, it will change from time to time because of machine breakdown, holidays and other factors. To create realistic production plans based on the capacity actually available at the time, a close working relationship must be maintained between the planning and production functions. The efficient working of another CAPM program, work-in-process, will also have a direct bearing on the integrity of volatile data supplied to the capacity planning program.

Product routeings. Like BOM, these consist exclusively of static data, ie details of all manufacturing operations which have to be performed and their sequence. This would normally be the responsibility of the process planning or production engineering section, who would maintain data on what was to be done, where and in what sequence, and also which tools and jigs were to be used. Much of this data will be created by this section, but care must be taken that process plans are followed on the shopfloor and that any *de facto* methods or routes are evaluated and incorporated in the routeing files if found to be superior to *de jure* ones.

Purchase ordering. The primary data held permanently on file is that of vendors and this would be maintained by the purchasing section. Vendor ratings are a key part of this data and should be regularly reviewed. Volatile data in this program will consist of the open purchase order details, ie quantities delivered, outstanding returned, etc, as well as tracking data on each purchase order, eg order date and due date. This too will be the responsibility of the purchasing section, although some of the data may be subject to direct input from other departments, for example goods inwards, or material control if the suggested orders from the MRP module causes purchase orders to be raised and recorded automatically. This implies a high degree of review and control of the systems operation by Purchasing staff.

Works orders. Works orders are a direct result of sales orders or are instigated by the production plan, and can be raised either by the Sales or Production Control Departments. The CAPM system may allow the creation of a works order directly from a sales order, in which case data will be transferred from one program to the other. Often the product terminology used by the Sales Department can differ from the more technical terms of production, and any data entered into the computer system must have the same meaning for all users. By the same token, the Sales Department may frequently need to access data on the status of individual works orders to enable customers to be kept informed, so there is a need for this to be constantly updated if a 'real time' system is to be achieved.

Work-in-process. The tracking of work-in-process is made possible by the constant gathering of data from the shopfloor and its entry into the computer system. Some of this data is then fed into the works order and the capacity planning and scheduling programs to update them. Shopfloor data collection can be automated, as in bar-code reading or machine monitoring systems, but the bulk of it is likely to remain manual for some time to come, and in being manual, there is great capacity for data errors. The Work-in-process program is a primary tool of the production control section and it is their responsibility to ensure the accuracy of the data entered into the system, by making shopfloor staff aware of the need for it and by regular data monitoring.

Costing. The gathering of actual costs of manufacture for comparison with standard or estimated costs is of vital importance to the efficient running of any manufacturing business and yet it is one of the most consistently neglected areas of all. Data must be accurate and timely to be of any use, and much of it will emanate from the Work-in-process program, eg set-up times, operation times, production quantities. Material costs will be computed from issue and usage records. Responsibility for data entered into the costing system will therefore fall upon three sections, production, material control and financial, the latter calculating and maintaining the overhead costs data. Both types of data are of equal importance, the static data, eg material costs, labour costs, power costs, and the volatile data which gives details of individual works orders or production batches. Systems for cost record maintenance should be set up and the accuracy of actual cost gathering regularly reviewed.

These are some of the main areas in which data has to be gathered and maintained in order for the CAPM system to work effectively and give its users the right information to make decisions and record the performance of the business. Late and inaccurate data in any part of a CAPM system weakens its efficiency and will eventually render it inoperable. Unrealistic sales forecasts and out-of-date costs make a nonsense of efforts made in planning and product pricing. Inaccurate BOM and routeings result in a high scrap rate and lengthened lead times, leading to increased costs and dissatisfied customers. The time spent in allocating responsibilities, drawing up systems for data maintenance and conducting systems audits will be repaid ten times over in accurate data and efficient operation.

Systems ownership

Just as there is a need for users to be consulted about the strengths and weaknesses of current systems, and their views on possible features and functionality to be included in the specification for the new CAPM systems, there is also a requirement for these same people to accept the new systems as being able to fulfil their operational needs, to adopt them as the sole method of working and to give them wholehearted support. In other words, each user must develop as strong a sense of systems ownership as he or she had with the old system, not only for those parts with which he or she comes into direct contact but also for the CAPM system as a whole. In order to achieve this, every effort must be made to show why the new systems are needed and what benefits they will bring, both in terms of greater efficiency and in relieving individuals of some of their mundane and duplicative tasks.

Changing attitudes is difficult at the best of times. People are suspicious of new ideas and methods, unsure of their own abilities in handling them and fearful of committing themselves to the unknown. If such a change can be brought about, the new systems will be taken up and supported enthusiastically, because staff will have had a hand in their specification and implementation and will see the advantages both for the business and for themselves. The only way in which this can occur, and it is a theme which cannot be stressed too often, is through education, training, adequate resources being made available for the implementation and an obvious commitment by senior management to the new philosophy. All of this must go hand-in-hand with a clear appreciation and knowledge of the principles which underlie any CAPM system, that is the planning and control of material and production. The project manager and the steering committee members have a clear role to play here. They must 'sell' the CAPM system to those people who will be required to make it work, the people who will be its sole support once implementation is complete and the project team disbanded.

If the new systems arc not accepted by most people at an early stage, or if there are serious problems with their implementation, then all sorts of negative influences come into play, in addition to the growing doubts about the abilities of senior executives to manage the enterprise. Those who had serious doubts about the efficacy of the new systems, whether ill-founded or not, will feel free to voice them and by doing so will start to undermine the efforts of others. People will begin to revert to their old systems, or an adaptation of them, with the excuse that "they worked all right for years". This in turn will lessen the integrity of the CAPM systems, and cause them to perform even worse than before. If people say that the new systems are no good, and then act accordingly, they will inevitably bring about that which they are predicting. It will be a self-fulfilling prophecy. This must not be allowed to happen, as it will inevitably lead to the failure of the CAPM project, which cannot but have a significant and detrimental effect on the whole business.

Monitoring key factors

You will recall that in Chapter Seven it was said that the whole premise on which the CAPM implementation should be based was that, following the implementation, your manufacturing business would be significantly improved. Of course, this in itself is totally inadequate to justify such major expenditure and upheaval in the company. A financial justification based on certain achievements is required, and these we called key targets. Such targets could cover a wide range of possibilities but those on which the return on investment calculations are to be based need to be expressed in financial terms. That is not to say that other, non-financial targets cannot be set, such as lower absenteeism and staff turnover, or increased morale, though even those might have a financial value attached to them.

Although most of the key targets likely to be set at the beginning of the CAPM project will be in those areas of activity which would in any event be monitored in any well-run manufacturing business, because they are of such particular significance to the success of the CAPM project they should be the subject of separate reports throughout the period chosen. This will highlight their importance and give people an added incentive towards their achievement. And there is little to be gained by saying, for instance, that a 40 per cent reduction in raw materials stocks at the end of two years is one of the targets. That is too far in the future and too large a figure to think of attaining. Better to draw up a series of smaller stock reductions, spread over the two year period, thus reducing the apparent size of the task and bringing each mini-target in turn within a recognizable timescale. These targets and the progress towards their attainment can be given in a 'CAPM Bulletin', which could be published at regular intervals throughout the implementation project and for as long after it as is thought necessary or of interest.

Post-implementation audit

An aspect of CAPM implementation which is often neglected or performed inadequately is the post-implementation systems audit. Ideally, this should be carried out for each sub-system or module immediately following its implementation. If this is not practical, then this task should be accomplished as soon as possible after the whole system is up and running. The responsibility for this lies with the project manager and the objective of it is to check that all procedures are being followed as laid down in the procedures manual and in the systems users manual provided by the vendor.

This initial audit, and more especially the subsequent audits which should be carried out twice a year, should allow for the fact that the users will almost certainly come up with 'better' ways of achieving desired results with the system. These may well be improvements, but they may equally be aberrations which will detract from operational efficiency and undermine the principles on which the computerized systems are based. Where any serious deviation from the approved procedures is found, it should be immediately discontinued and the approved method reinstated, otherwise it may start a process of gradual drift which will eventually leave a company's manufacturing systems in worse shape than when the CAPM project was started. If the innovations put forward by a user are good, credit should be given and the new methods entered in the procedures manual. If unacceptable, credit should at least be given for the effort made, and a willingness expressed to consider any other 'improvements' which the user might devise. From time to time, CAPM users discover abilities within such systems that are unknown to those who created the systems, and someone gaining the intimate knowledge of a system which a frequent user does can often make for significant improvements to the original procedures.

Additional systems

For the purposes of this book, Computer-aided production management (CAPM) was defined at the outset as all of those computerized systems which could be used for administrative purposes, from SOP through inventory control and purchasing to production planning and control. One of the reasons for including certain functions or modules (and excluding others) is because they are the ones commonly found in package systems with which this book has been primarily concerned. The systems offered by different vendors can vary considerably, not only in the modules they offer but also in the functionality and features within modules which are ostensibly the same. It is because of this that the investigation, specification and selection procedures are so important to the success of any CAPM project.

Having successfully implemented an integrated CAPM system, the company should then consider the possibilities of extending that system by the addition of other, peripheral systems which will further enhance administrative ability and give cost-effective improvements in the manufacturing and ancillary functions. Some of these systems may already be in operation in a 'stand-alone' mode, or may have been operational even before CAPM was considered as a possibility; CAD is one system which is often encountered. While such systems can work well on their own, as in any type of computer integration, they can bring greater benefits to the users if they are part of a larger manufacturing system, from which they can extract data and into which they can enter data to be used in other sectors of the system. If they are not linked electronically, communication between programs must be manual, with that method's inherent slowness and proneness to error.

Three of the most common systems in this category are:

Computer-aided design (CAD). This is the use of a computer system to design the products to be made by the company, with facility to create, store, retrieve and analyse geometric models and parts lists or BOM. It is the latter which is of relevance to the process of integration. Provided the two systems, CAD and CAPM are compatible, a link can be made whereby the materials data from any product designed on the CAD system can be transferred to the BOM module in CAPM, thus reducing the possibility of error and saving a considerable amount of time.

Computer-aided estimating (CAE). There are computerized systems for the estimation of costs, including design, manufacturing and distribution (where appropriate) costs, enabling the user to draw on a database of cost elements, perform calculations and produce a product selling price for customer quotation purposes. Such systems are especially useful in a 'make-to-order' environment, where comprehensive estimates of complex products have to be carried out for every quotation. CAE programs often operate in a 'stand-alone' mode but are increasingly available in combination with Computer-aided process planning (CAPP), as they complement each other, the CAE part being a shadow of the later and more detailed process plan.

Computer-aided process planning (CAPP). This is a computerized system for the creation, storage and retrieval of production methods. Its primary output is the process plan or product routeing which shows the operations which must be carried out to effect manufacture of the product, their sequence and duration, as well as other information such as the machines and tooling to be used. In some systems where a CAE program is also used, data from this can be extracted and used as a basis for creating the process plan which in turn can be transferred to the product routeings files for issue to the shopfloor.

Systems such as these may not be applicable to the methods of manufacture used in your company, and if they are, there could be reasons why they should not be integrated with the CAPM system. In the same manner as a CAPM system, if a prima-facie case can be made out for one or more of them, it is worth investing some time and effort to investigate their potential, provided that a proper evaluation and cost justification is carried out before a purchase decision is taken. Of course management should always be ready to investigate any enhancements or additions to the CAPM or allied systems which are available, and should never be content to rest on their laurels. You can be sure that competitors will be continually looking at developments in the area of computerized manufacturing and making an investment wherever they think a competitive advantage can be gained. The process is never-ending. Computer technology and systems development is such that new and more sophisticated products frequently come onto the market, so that the 'state-of-the-art' CAPM system of three or four years ago is already beginning to look a little old and outmoded.

CHAPTER 13

Starting Over

Distasteful as it may be to contemplate, it must be recognized that, even in a well-regulated project, things can go wrong in a CAPM implementation or during its subsequent use. These can range from minor hiccups in a particular module or sub-system, such as difficulty in achieving the required accuracy in inventory data, to such critical failure in key sectors that the whole system has to be abandoned. This latter scenario is extreme and thankfully is rarely encountered, yet it does happen from time to time and usually with disastrous consequences for the company concerned, even to the extent of closing down the business.

A much more common situation is where some of the CAPM programs are operating satisfactorily, some are limping along and giving more trouble than they are worth, while others were either never implemented at all or proved so difficult in implementation or operation that they were quickly abandoned. The large investment made in hardware, software and implementation effort is conveniently forgotten and most people readily adopt the excuse that the unused programs were never really appropriate to the company's requirements. This takes place in company after company across the manufacturing sector, with the blame for failure being placed on the hardware, the software, the systems vendor, the uniqueness of the company's business, the contrariness of customers or the unreliability of vendors, in fact on anything except where it should lie – the people who chose the CAPM system and subsequently planned and managed its implementation. It is here that the pitfalls lie and the mistakes are made, and it is with the avoidance of them that this book has been concerned. Of course, many companies will tell you that they have installed an integrated CAPM system, and to the casual observer everything looks wonderful. However, closer inspection will reveal that although the system might be installed it is certainly not fully effective.

There can be many signs of a poorly-run and ineffective system. Some of them are obvious, such as a consistent failure to meet delivery dates or inventory levels which are well out of line with requirements. Other signs are not so obvious, such as outdated BOM or inaccurate management information. If you find that inventory accuracy is as bad as ever it was under the old system, and the output from MRP is largely disregarded as irrelevant while informal manual systems flourish on every hand, you can be sure that major problems, both operational and psychological, lie ahead. The system has been substantially rejected by many of the staff as a failure or at least as having limited relevance to their daily operational needs.

The reasons for failure

So what do you do if you have had an unsuccessful implementation or find yourself as a manager having to take over responsibility for a CAPM system which is running substantially below par? Quite simply, you have to start over again using the principles and practices given in preceding chapters. Before solutions to the problem can be formulated, the reasons for failure must first be determined. It might be that there is one single cause for the systems failure, such as totally wrong applications software having been chosen, so that even the best implementational efforts are to no avail. But this is unlikely. It is much more common to find that there are a number of reasons, the cumulative effect of which is to leave the CAPM system substantially inoperative or with output which is at odds with the systems users' requirements. Below is a list of common reasons for failure. All of them are found frequently and in various combinations:

- Poor education and training of manufacturing staff
- Lack of commitment by management and staff
- Inadequate resources given to the project
- Not enough 'people involvement' either in the selection or implementation processes
- Insufficient data integrity
- Inability to change from informal to formal systems, ie poor systems discipline
- The wrong software chosen
- Inadequate project planning and management
- Lack of knowledge of basic manufacturing principles, eg inventory control, production control, costing
- Inadequate CAPM expertise, either from internal personnel or from an external consultant.

Let us briefly examine some of these causes so that we can determine how they come about and what can be done to prevent or remedy them.

Poor education and training. The amount of education and training required is often underestimated. People who are going to run and use the system must be aware of the principles under which it works, the benefits to the company of implementation and the procedures to be followed in order to make the software work to their satisfaction. There is simply no point in presenting the users with the hardware, software and the User Manual and telling them to 'Get on with it'. All you will get is a system which does not work and a group of resentful employees. The investment made in good education and training will repay itself ten times over. If your company missed out on it first time around then you must start at the beginning with education and training sessions, assuming little, if any, knowledge on the part of the systems users, and making sure that everyone understands what is to be done, how it is to be done and why it *must* be done.

Lack of commitment. If the senior management of an organization decides to spend a considerable amount of its resources on implementing a CAPM system, it would seem reasonable to expect that they were committed to the project. Unfortunately this is not always the case. These are often the same members of management who fail to involve their manufacturing people in the selection of the systems, and when things start going wrong they blame it on the intransigence of their staff. The underlying problem is that this type of management does not want to invest time and effort in determining the proper systems solution to their problems and painstakingly move towards it. What they want is a 'quick fix'. They have been sold the idea of MRP or JIT or some such and they *know* it is the answer they have been looking for. They have done the difficult bit in deciding the future direction of manufacturing philosophy and systems. It is now up to the staff to make the thing work. But when the going gets tough, and the staff look to the management for leadership and commitment, it is not to be found. Therefore it is only to be expected that the staff will lose whatever commitment they had and the skids will be under the project. This is one of the most difficult problems to remedy, as those being asked to make the system work will have lost faith in it (if they ever had any), and this appears to be justified by the fact that it does not do what is required of it. The only way of retrieving a situation such as this is to relaunch the whole CAPM project, with management playing more prominent roles than formerly, showing clear and unequivocal commitment. It will not be easy to raise enthusiasm for what may be thought of as a white elephant, but it must be accomplished otherwise the CAPM system will have to be abandoned completely.

Inadequate resources. CAPM systems are difficult enough to implement without further reducing the chances by trying to conduct the project on the cheap. While flinging money at it will not of itself achieve very much, when the CAPM project budget is being drawn up, there should be adequate provision made for such things as education, training, consultancy and temporary labour. Nor can it be expected that a cheaper and less sophisticated CAPM system will give all of those features and functionality which the company would like to acquire, such as material traceability, contract costing or 'what-if' capacity planning. From limited resources it is better if a less sophisticated system is purchased, allowing enough money for training and consultancy, than that all available money is spent on the best possible system which then lies idle because no-one knows how to operate it properly. On determining that lack of resources has been the cause of systems failure or poor performance, there is no other course of action possible but to put in more resources. If the CAPM system or major parts of it are not operational, then these need to be started again from the beginning, making sure that this time everyone is properly trained in their use and enough manpower is available to ensure the accuracy of data before it is entered onto the files. If some or all of the modules are running but are imperfectly understood and giving poor results, then a program must be laid down for remedial action, eg gradual improvement of data accuracy, with the appropriate resources made available.

Insufficient data integrity. This is primarily caused by lack of systems discipline, where users fall back into the old, informal habits where many numbers were estimates with a bit added for good measure. The most obvious places in which this will occur will be inventory records and transactions, BOM and shopfloor performance figures. If these inaccuracies become widespread, the data being produced by the CAPM system will bear no relationship to what is actually happening in the various manufacturing sections of the company and the system will become unworkable, or at best will be a series of actions maintained for the sake of appearances, while the real work of planning and control is carried out by the informal systems. In order to get such a system back on the rails it will be necessary to appoint a project manager responsible for drawing up a plan of action to restore data accuracy and to see that it is carried out. The procedures used in each section of the system must be checked to establish the causes of poor data integrity and specific action taken in each case to amend the procedures to overcome this. A general exhortation to greater accuracy will do nothing to retrieve the situation.

The wrong software chosen. It is sad but true that in many companies it will only be realized that the wrong software has been chosen when someone on a training course asks about a particular area of functionality or tries to carry out certain actions on the system, only to find that it does not have the particular facility in question. This may be something quite vital, such as lot traceability or job costing. On the contrary, the company might have purchased an

MRP-based system when they had no need of that technique and have paid for something that they are never going to use. Such things are the result of poor or non-existent systems specification, inadequate vetting of tenders and lack of advice from an experienced person. The remedial action to be taken in this instance will depend on the degree of mismatch between the CAPM system installed and your company's requirements. Minor variances could perhaps be rectified by some 'tailoring' carried out by the systems vendor, otherwise it will have to be left and treated as a minor if permanent annoyance. An individual program or module, which is to a large degree inadequate, could possibly be replaced by one from another suite of programs, although frequently this is not possible due to incompatibility of the two systems. Otherwise, the problem will have to be overcome by the use of additional manual procedures. In the worst case, where a number of the programs are seriously deficient, the only answer is to replace the whole system, because continued use of such a system will cause more problems than it solves and may end up by seriously damaging the business.

Inadequate project planning. Along with lack of education and training, this is one of the most common reasons for a poor CAPM implementation. This will be evident from the excessive length of time taken to install the various programs, false starts and program implementations abandoned halfway through because there has been no data preparation or user education. Even in the smaller company implementing a modest manufacturing system, detailed planning and management is required. Things will not simply happen of their own accord, and once events have been planned to take place the progress towards the target date must be closely monitored, with named individuals being held responsible for each task to be carried out. Where it becomes evident that the planning or control has been inadequate, the whole project or the parts affected should be stopped while stock is taken and a proper plan is formulated. Lack of control of the project is caused by insufficient priority being given to it, either because a project manager has not been appointed, has not given enough time to it, or enthusiasm and motivation have been allowed to wane. Project planning of itself can make the difference between success and failure. A good plan can develop a momentum of its own, with each task and phase leading on logically to the next one, accompanied by the provision of data and facilities at the right time.

Lack of knowledge of basic manufacturing principles. This is a more common contributory factor in CAPM implementation failure than is generally acknowledged. Without a change of attitude on the part of those people running an inefficient manufacturing company, and a conscious attempt to broaden their knowledge, there is no reason to suppose that a computer-aided manufacturing system will be administered any better than a manual one. If the systems users are not conversant with the principles and practice of inventory control, production control and costing, for example, they will go through the motions taught them by the system vendor, but there will be little understanding. This should be part of the preimplementation process, when the educational and training needs of individual users should be determined and the appropriate instruction arranged. The lack of such knowledge is likely to become apparent during computer systems training by the vendor, where difficulty will be experienced in understanding the terminology and the techniques. It is not the function of the vendor to teach the principles of production control or material requirements planning, and shortcomings uncovered will need to be remedied as soon as possible, otherwise the CAPM system will be poorly run and will not give the expected results.

Inadequate CAPM expertise. Companies often make the mistake of thinking that because they have been running their business for years, they know what they want from a CAPM system. Of course, in many areas they will do, but unless there is someone experienced in CAPM to ask the right questions, the company is likely to end with the wrong system, or at least one which is a poor fit to their requirements. Similarly, a lack of CAPM implementation knowledge may lengthen the process and allow avoidable mistakes to occur. Lack of CAPM experience (although it might not be recognized as a problem at this juncture) can be seen where companies spend months evaluating many systems by reading literature, talking to representatives and having demonstrations. They have no yardstick (specification) against which to measure each system, and by the time they have seen the twenty-third one they cannot possibly compare it with the first. When it comes to the planning of the project, unrealistic time estimates are made for the various implementation tasks, training needs are not taken into account and data accuracy is often neglected. Sufficient knowledge of CAPM can be instated in the company either by recruiting someone who already has it or having someone who is a member of the organization, acquire it. This latter can be effective if put in motion before the start of the project but too little and too late after the implementation runs into serious trouble. Then the only practical remedy is to call in a consultant to give advice. It might appear to be expensive at the time, yet in the long run it will be cheaper than trying to go it alone and eventually having to abandon the whole project.

Damage limitation

When it is obvious that a CAPM implementation has gone wrong, either in whole or in part, immediate steps should be taken to effect damage limitation. This has to take place on two fronts, namely operational and psychological. The first and most important is the operational aspect. At all costs, the business must be kept running smoothly, and the effect a poor or stalled implementation can have on manufacturing operations must never be underestimated. At best it will be disruptive and at worst it can cause a complete operational shutdown which is usually temporary but can be permanent.

Operational considerations

At some point a decision has to be made as to whether the problem systems are to be suspended and replaced with the previous ones, or whether they should be kept running with manual assistance while a recovery plan is evolved and put into action. This will depend on the extent of the problem. The key question will be "Which course of action will best maintain the smooth running of the manufacturing operations?" There is a lot to be said for trying to keep the computer systems running, however poorly they are performing, as it is difficult to crank up enough enthusiasm and motivation for a relaunch once systems have been shut down and therefore been shown to be inoperable, albeit in a particular set of circumstances. In some instances, system users may only be going through the motions, with little of value being produced from some of the programs which they are running. If this is allowed to go on for any length of time, then any credibility which the system might once have had will be totally lost, and managerial ability will also be severely questioned. Solutions to the problem must be quick and effective, with emphasis being placed on the failure of planning and the management of resources, rather than the unsuitability of the software or the incompetence of the users. (Naturally, if one or other is incompetent, the software should be thrown out and the users replaced.) Suspension of all or part of the CAPM system should be a last resort: it is relatively easy to do, but it makes for a long climb back, and as often as not the reinstatement never takes place.

Psychological considerations

The second aspect which must be considered is the psychological one, and this has been touched upon in the preceding section. As with a first-time implementation, the perceptions of those implementing and using the system are of prime importance. They will have put a lot of hard work into an implementation which will now appear to have been a failure. They will know that they have done what was asked of them, so any blame will be laid squarely with the project management in particular and senior management in general. It will be the responsibility of those persons to come up with the solution to the problem. If that means replacing the project manager, the steering committee or both, then that is what has to be done for there is no sense in expecting success the second time around by trying to go down the same path in the same manner as before.

Replanning and raising enthusiasm to start again

Positive steps should be taken to maintain people's faith in the system and their willingness to make a further effort to achieve success. This should be done by:

- reiterating the benefits which formed the original justification for implementing the system and stressing that they are still valid
- showing the benefits of those parts of the system which have been successfully implemented
- explaining that CAPM implementation is a complex undertaking and is seldom trouble-free
- explaining why success has not been complete and showing what has been planned to recover the situation
- restating management's commitment to the project.

Implementations of CAPM systems are rarely complete and unqualified successes, because like so many other business activities, much of it depends on prediction of one sort or another. The software will be a good fit for the company's manufacturing needs – provided the business does not change significantly. Based on experience, assumptions are made about the reaction of the workforce and these may not turn out to be correct in every respect. The difficulties of gathering and checking data may be underestimated because the task has never been done before. There are numerous things, both foreseen and unforeseen which can go wrong. This does not mean that the project should never be tackled, nor does it mean that if success is not instant and complete the system should be abandoned, as has happened so often in manufacturing organizations. CAPM systems are regularly implemented with success in companies across the whole manufacturing spectrum, and yet in other organizations there are systems which are wholly or partly moribund, having consumed scarce resources and tied up expensive and much-needed capital. Provided that the system chosen is appropriate for the manufacturing needs of the business, a stalled implementation can be restarted. It takes time and patience and effort. The organization must be convinced of its efficacy, they must pull together as a team and the three cardinal points must always be observed: commitment, project management and adequate resources.

GLOSSARY

ABC Classification: a method of classifying each inventory item according to its rate of usage and value.

Allocated stock: raw materials or finished goods which have been reserved from physical stock against a particular works order or customer order.

Alternative route: another method of manufacturing a product, generally used when the optimum route cannot be followed.

Applications software: computer programs designed for specific applications, such as inventory control, production control or costing.

Arrears (backlog): sales orders which have been received but have missed their due shipment dates.

Assembly: a finished product, consisting of some combination of raw materials, components and sub-assemblies.

Automatic rescheduling: where the computer changes due dates on scheduled receipts (ie open production and purchase orders) to correspond to changes of demand.

Available to promise: uncommitted inventory or planned production, sometimes calculated from the master production schedule (MPS).

Backflushing (Simultaneous issue and receipt): the post-production calculation and deduction from inventory records of materials used, based on the quantity of end items manufactured.

Back-log, see **Arrears.**

Backwards scheduling: the calculation of operation start and due dates, commencing with the order shipping date and working backwards.

Batch: (Lot) a quantity of material or components which are purchased or processed in one lot.

Bill of material (BOM): a hierarchical list of the raw materials, components and sub-assemblies required to manufacture one item, often including costs.

Bin card: a record of stock movements and balances, one for each material or component type, usually attached to the inventory container.

Binning: the placing in storage locations of materials received, whether raw materials, part-finished components or finished products.

Blanket order (Call-off; Vendor schedule): an order placed by the manufacturer on the vendor, or by the customer on the manufacturer, detailing delivery quantities over a number of periods. Often incorporates a rolling requirements forecast eg one month firm, two months variable.

Bucketed system: a method used in materials requirements planning (MRP) of gathering time-phased data into periods of time (buckets), eg daily, weekly, monthly.

Bucketless system: the creation and maintenance of dated records for all time-phased data in MRP, in contrast to the **Bucketed System.**

Buffer stock, see **Safety stock.**

Business plan: a corporate-level schedule of planned commercial, financial and manufacturing activities, usually covering a period of 12 months in detail and a further 4 years in outline.

CAD (computer-aided-design): the use of a computer for the creation, manipulation, storage and retrieval of product designs.

CAE (computer-aided estimating): a computer system for the calculation of job or contract estimates, using previous similar estimates on file, directly input data or data from other modules such as Inventory Control or Purchase Order Processing.

Calendar (Shop calendar): a calendar within the CAPM suite of programs used in capacity planning and scheduling, is configured to show working and non-working days in a manufacturing plant.

Capacity: the productive ability of a given manufacturing facility.

Capacity requirements planning: the determination of production capacity and its allocation to open works orders, in terms of labour and machines available at each work centre.

CAPP (Computer-aided process planning): a computer system which facilitates the creation, storage and retrieval of production methods, including the machines, tooling, operation sequence and timing.

Closed-loop system: any system which provides feedback of results from actions so that modifications can be made where necessary, prior to further action.

Component: a discrete item manufactured from one raw material, eg a bolt

Cycle counting (Perpetual inventory): a system of physical checking of inventory items in which a daily count of specified items is carried out and reconciled with inventory records. Often replaces periodic, full, physical inventory checks.

Demand: a requirement for raw material, sub-assemblies or finished assembly.

Dependent demand: in an MRP system, demand for any sub-assembly, component or raw material which is dependent upon demand for the item of which it is a part.

End item: any finished product, assembly or individual part occurring at the highest level in the product structure or as a spare part.

Explosion: the breaking down of a final assembly, by use of its bill of material, into its component parts and raw materials.

Finite scheduling/loading: the scheduling of workload onto the shopfloor according to the amount of capacity available at each work centre in a finite time.

Firm planned order: An order which has been planned for a specific quantity and time period, and one which cannot be changed automatically by the computer. The MPS is normally stated in terms of firm planned orders.

First in, first out (FIFO): a material costing system in which the unit cost of the oldest extant material is used.

Fixed order quantity: where the same quantity of material is ordered each time from a vendor.

Floor stocks: stocks of materials or components which are held not in the stores but adjacent to a work centre, for ease of access.

Flow process (Continuous manufacturing): the manufacture of products, often indiscrete, in a constant process, ie without queue time between operations.

Forecast: a quantified prediction, usually based on projected trends and/or market intelligence, of future events in a specific area of activity, eg sales, production.

Forward scheduling: the determination of a completion date, commencing at a given start date and proceeding through each manufacturing operation. (See **Backward scheduling**)

Free issue: material supplied free of charge by a customer for use in the manufacture of products for that customer.

Free stock: the quantity of unallocated stock which is available for use.

Gross requirements: in an MRP system, the calculation of material demand, without reference to stock-on-hand or planned receipts. (See **Net requirements**)

Independent demand: in an MRP system, demand for any material or sub-assembly not dependent upon demand for a higher level item, eg spare parts.

Infinite scheduling/loading: the scheduling of workload onto the shopfloor regardless of the available capacity at each work centre.

Inventory: the stock of materials held to facilitate production, or of finished goods held to fulfil sales orders.

Inventory control: the method of regulating materials or finished goods in order to maximize availability and minimize cost.

Item master record: the constant data maintained for each raw material, component, sub-assembly or final assembly recorded in the inventory files.

Job card: a written instruction for the manufacture of a specific item, batch of items, or to carry out one production operation.

Job shop: a facility which manufactures made-to-order products singly or in small batches.

Just-in-time (JIT): a manufacturing philosophy, perfected in Japan, which aims at the continual uncovering and permanent solution of manufacturing problems.

Kanban: a Japanese word, meaning 'sign', applied to a production technique in which an operation cannot take place without receipt of a card from the previous operation.

Kitting (Kit marshalling): the process of gathering all the materials required to manufacture a given quantity of product. (See **Trial kitting**)

Last in, first out (LIFO): a material costing system in which the latest unit cost of material is used.

Lead time: the normal or average time which elapses between the start of a process or routine and its completion, eg between placing a purchase order on a vendor and receiving the material.

Level: in a bill of material, the point in the hierarchical structure at which a given material occurs.

Load: the amount of work scheduled for a work centre, individual machine or labour resource, stated in terms of hours or units of production.

Local area network (LAN): the linking of personal computers for the purpose of sharing data from a common database.

Lost time: production time, of either labour or machine, which is unable to be used due to some unplanned occurrence, eg machine breakdown.

Lot, see **Batch.**

Made-to-order: a product only manufactured in response to a specific customer order. (See **Made-to-stock**)

Made-to-stock: a product made in such quantity and frequency as to allow it to be held and supplied from stock.

Manufacturing resource planning (MRP II): a computerized and integrated manufacturing system covering all production, sales and financial administration systems.

Master production schedule (MPS): the planned output of finished products, by quantity and date, which is checked by rough-cut capacity planning before becoming the major input for the MRP module.

Materails requirements planning (MRP): a technique used to calculate materials requirements for manufacturing, drawing data from inventory control, bills of material and production schedule systems. Can be run manually, but normally computerized due to the amount of data which has to be handled.

Net change MRP: a continuous or periodic method of calculating materials requirements, following changes in demand or supply, in which only those items affected by the change are included.

Net requirements: in MRP, gross material requirements minus stock-on-hand and planned receipts.

Offset lead time: in MRP, the period of time between the release of a works or purchase order and its due date.

Open order: a works, purchase or customer order which is as yet unfulfilled.

Operating software: the computer programs which manage the systems resources, such as devices, memory and applications programs.

Order book: the amount of sales orders on hand, expressed in monetary terms or units of production.

Order entry: the input of sales order details into the sales order processing system.

Part-finished items: components, sub-assemblies or assemblies which are held in stock in an unfinished state so that demand for different finished options can more quickly be fulfilled.

Pegging: in MRP, a method of tracing the gross requirement for a material or item back to where the demand was created.

Picking: the extraction of materials or finished products from stock against a list of requirements such as a kit list, material requisition or picking list.

Picking list: a list of items to be taken from stock for despatch or manufacturing purposes.

Planned orders: order quantities and dates suggested by MRP, from calculated net requirements, which can be used as input data for the capacity requirements planning system.

Planning horizon: in an MRP system, the number of time periods between the present and some future date, over which material requirements can be planned.

Pre-allocated stock: raw materials or finished goods which have been promised to a works order or customer order, from stock which is not on hand but is on order.

Production planning: the detailed arrangement of production activities and resources in order to manufacture the required items.

Product structure, see **Bill of material.**

Queue time: the period of time an item or batch of items awaits processing at one or more work centres.

Regenerative MRP: a method of calculating material requirements following changes in demand or supply, in which all items are included.

Re-order level (ROL): the pre-determined inventory quantity for a material or item at which a replenishment order is triggered.

Re-order quantity (ROQ): the pre-determined quantity of a material or item which is the subject of a replenishment order.

Rescheduling: calculating the sequence of jobs through work centres following changes in demand or resources.

Resource requirements planning, see **Rough-cut capacity planning.**

Rough-cut capacity planning: the testing of the MPS or production plan feasibility against key production resources.

Routeing: a list of those manufacturing operations in the sequence in which they are to be carried out for the production of an item or batch of items.

Run time: the time allowed for a production operation to take place on one item or a batch of items.

Safety stock: a pre-determined quantity of an item held in inventory, in addition to that allowed to cover replenishment lead-time, to ensure against stockout due to unpredictable supply and demand changes.

Scheduled receipts: open production and purchase orders at their due date, treated by MRP as available inventory for that time period.

Scrap factor: the allowance made for items produced below standard, and therefore unusable.

Set-up time: the time allowed to prepare a production facility to carry out an operation on a specific type of item.

Shopfloor control: the process of monitoring and controlling the progress of works orders through production operations.

Shopfloor data collection: the manual or computerized gathering of information on the status of works orders in the production process.

Simulation ("What-if" analysis): the evaluation of alternative plans, using a computer program such as Shopfloor Scheduling.

Simultaneous issue and receipt, see **Backflushing.**

Spares: items sold as replacement parts on a finished product. In MRP terms they are of independent demand as they do not depend on demand for a higher level BOM item.

Stock on hand: the physical inventory of an item, which may consist of allocated stock and/or free stock.

Stock turn: a measure of inventory efficiency; in monetary terms, the annual materials usage divided by the average stockholding.

Tailoring: the adaptation of package computer applications programs in order to provide a better 'fit' to specified requirements.

Time bucket: in MRP, the summarizing of small time periods into a larger one for the purpose of stating gross requirements.

Time fence: the point in time at which limitations on action come into force, eg changes to the MPS.

Trial kitting: the comparison of material requirements for a batch of production with the inventory records, in order to determine the level of material availability.

Two-bin system: a manual inventory control system, normally used for items of small unit value, in which a purchase requisition is raised when a new batch is commenced.

Vendor schedule, see **Blanket order.**

"What-if" analysis, see **Simulation.**

Work centre: a unit of productive capacity composed of people and/or machines, so configured as to facilitate production and its planning and control.

Work-in-process: jobs which have been started in the production cycle but have not yet reached completion.

Work-to list: a list of jobs in priority sequence, issued to a work centre.

Yield: the amount of output of acceptable quality from a production process, compared to the material input.

APPENDIX I:

INVITATION TO TENDER

Computer Systems Specification

for

XYZ Co
Long Road
Birmingham

Contents

1. INTRODUCTION

Your company is invited to tender for the supply, delivery, installation and support services of a complete CAPM system to meet the specification given below.

The tender should include not only the hardware and software details and costs, but also any other costs which may be involved, eg training, support.

In addition, the tender should include an 'overview' of your company, with particular reference to your qualifications to supply the hardware, software and services to XYZ Co.

You are expected to supply details of suitable reference sites which could be contacted directly by XYZ Co. However, no such contacts would be made without prior arrangement with yourselves.

The tender documentation should reach the persons named below no later than four weeks from the date of this invitation to tender.

a) Mr T Smith   (1 copy)
    Manufacturing Manager
    XYZ Co
    Long Road
    Birmingham

b) Mr F Brown   (1 copy)
    Manufacturing Systems Consultant
    Brown and Jones Associates
    Short Road
    Birmingham

The XYZ Co designs and manufactures a range of injection-moulded, automotive components, a large proportion of which have metal inserts. This range of products has expanded over recent years with the company now offering a sub-contract manufacturing facility to other organizations. The market is sensitive to delivery performance and lead times are, of necessity, short. As a result of this, some components are produced against a sales forecast which may vary considerably in accuracy, due to frequently changing customer demand.

In addition to the manufacture of plastic components, the company undertakes some assembly and transfer-printing work and offers a variety of finished packaging options.

The administration and production systems within the company have been developed over a number of years and are largely manual. The only computer equipment currently used is an IBM PC for word processing and a simple accounts system. There is no experience of computer systems within the manufacturing department.

The production control and costing systems have been in use for many years and do not provide information consistent with full control of the production operation. While the current systems have served the company well in the past, they have now been outgrown and shortcomings are apparent in a number of key areas. A point has now been reached where better systems are required to maintain and improve control over the business. It is the company's intention to commence with a MRP system and over a period of two to three years to move towards an MRP II environment.

2. TENDER REQUIREMENTS

Answers to *all* of the following questions should be included in your proposals.

2.1 Hardware

Proposed configuration costs? (excluding VAT)
Timing: delivery of hardware?
How much processor core is occupied by executive and operating systems and therefore is not available for applications?
What is the calculated disk storage capacity required to store the volumes given in the specification? How does this relate to the storage proposed?
Can the configuration be upgraded:
– processor
– peripherally (ie extra VDUs, additional memory storage)
Examples of subsequent phased enhancement costs?
What is the method for security copying of data, floppy disk, tape, removable hard disk?
Are all the pieces of hardware in current use? Give examples.
Is the equipment compatible with other systems? Give examples.
If you are not the manufacturer, then who is and who takes full responsibility?
What purchase options are available: outright sale, lease, hire purchase? (Give leasing rates if appropriate and the name of the finance company.)

2.2 Applications software

Which operating software options are available for the CAPM system proposed?
On what points do the package programs offered differ from the specification in this invitation to tender?
Timing: delivery of software?
Where a feature is not included in your system, please state the cost of

implementing the feature either by:
– tailoring of the program, or where this is not possible
– a specially written program.
Who will carry out the amendment?
By which companies are the proposed systems used?
Can they be seen and the users spoken to?
(These users should be in a similar industry to ourselves, in terms of product type, size of operation, manufacturing methods, etc.)
If you are offering custom-written software, is your company writing this or will it be sub-contracted to some other software house?
Who wrote the applications programs and who owns the copyright to them?
Is the source code available?
Is your organization a licensee or distributor of the CAPM systems which you are offering?
In what language is the applications software written?
What after-sales support is offered?
At which office is this support based?
Can the system run word processing and spreadsheets?
Can the system support/interface with telex, fax, office automation?

2.3 Maintenance

Annual costs (excluding VAT) – hardware and software?
Insurance costs?
Warranty period?
Who will carry out maintenance?
Where is your local maintenance centre?
Ratio of customer sites/engineers?
Response time for breakdowns?
Policy on out-of-hours calls?
Procedure if down-time exceeds one day?

2.4 Installation

Costs of installation?
Cost of hardware delivery?
Are there any special requirements, eg special mains supply, clean air, air conditioning, heat dissipation, special fittings/fixtures, floors, etc?

2.5 Training and implementation

Recommended implementation plan?
Definition of implementation responsibilities?
Cost of implementation?
What training is offered? Give costs and location.
Are there training facilities for different levels of user, eg operator, supervision, management?

2.6 Contractual terms

Please supply specimens of all relevant contracts.
Please give details of any arrangements available which guarantee the performance of your proposals.
What is your company's contractual policy on:
– system acceptance tests
– price revisions
– delivery dates
– enhancements (hardware and software)?
Insurance liabilities?
Payment terms?
Third party consumable supplier policy?
Buy-back and trade-in terms?

3. SYSTEMS SPECIFICATION

3.1 Overview

The company wishes to install a fully-integrated CAPM system covering the following applications areas:

- Sales order processing and invoicing
- Inventory control
- Materials requirements planning (MRP)
- Production planning and control
- Purchase order processing
- Costing.

The requirements for each area of activity are described below. Where possible, standard package programs should be offered, with 'tailoring' to meet specific requirements. The following should be used as a check list to indicate feature availability.

The system must be resilient enough to cope with varying levels of activity, with fast response even under pressure. It must be multi-user, with record-locking facility.

Full documentation and operator/user guides should be available for all modules supplied, including any 'tailoring' which has been carried out.

In general terms, XYZ Co requires a computer system which will carry it through the next ten years. Your company should therefore be prepared to give assurances that the system offered will meet this requirement by means of revisions and upgrades. The XYZ Co is looking for a system which will enable them to protect their investment in both hardware and software over this period.

3.2 Sales order processing and invoicing

The following features are required of the sales order processing and invoicing system:

166

1. On-line insertions, deletions, amendments and enquiries on sales orders.
2. Display of customer details at order input, including credit status.
3. Ability to handle blanket or scheduled orders and order call-offs.
4. Display of pricing and customer discount details.
5. Orders may be entered unpriced and prices entered at a later stage, up to the time of invoice printing.
6. Automatic updating of finished stock status on entry of a firm order.
7. Printing of order acknowledgements, including details of any arrears.
8. Printing of advice notes, with part-shipment facility.
9. Printing of invoices, as required (ie not necessarily at the same time as advice note).
10. Access to works order data so that delivery dates can be quoted during order input, or assessment of percentage order completion can be given to the customer.
11. Automatic release of arrears, when required, on receipt of finished goods into stock.
12. Individual orders or part orders printed for priority delivery, while the remaining part orders are held for scheduled delivery.
13. Reports of due/overdue orders and of all outstanding sales orders by customer, product type, giving details of order number, customer, quantity, part number and due date.
14. Invoice valuation.
15. Printing of pro-forma invoices.
16. Interfaces with Inventory Control and Accounts Receivable modules.
17. Free format text at sales order and individual line level.
18. Sales analysis by product line/type in terms of volume and value – current period, last period, same period last year, year-to-date, previous year (as required).
19. Sales analysis by customer in terms of volume and value – by part number/type, current period, etc.
20. Sales analysis by sales area/sales representative – by customer, by part number/type, current period, etc.
21. Profit analysis by customer, by part number/type, in quantity and value, cost of goods sold, gross profits in amounts and percentages, for current period, etc.
22. Sales report – total sales and costs against budgets, for current period, etc.

The last five points do not constitute a comprehensive list but merely illustrate the type and range of report requirements. It is therefore necessary that the system includes an applications report generator which will enable the users to specify and produce reports

167

of this nature, including simple mathematical functions, such as sub-totals, totals, averages, percentages, etc.

3.3 Product data management

This system should cover bills of material (BOM) structures and routings, (including machines, tools and work centres) and should have the following features:

1. On-line insertions, deletions, amendments and enquiries on BOMs and Routeings.
2. The ability to specify a 'mass change' of a component on all relevant BOMs.
3. The ability to create a BOM or routeing by the 'same as/except for' method.
4. The ability to specify a component part change by effectivity dates.
5. Single and multi-level retrieval of product data.
6. The ability to handle phantom assemblies.
7. A costed Bill of material/labour for each part on file.
8. An indented parts list by component part.
9. A 'where-used' report for any given component part.
10. The ability to hold an alternative route against each part.
11. Ability to define which operators and machines are available, and the limitations of which operators can operate which machines. A preference rating of an operator for a machine type, and an efficiency rating for that machine.

3.4 Inventory control

A comprehensive inventory control system is required which will handle raw materials, spares and finished goods, and will include the following features:

1. Interfaces with Sales Order Processing, MRP, Purchase Order Processing and Costing modules.
2. On-line additions, deletions, amendments and enquiries.
3. Item master details to be held on file for each item:

- inventory identity/part number
- material specification
- description
- supply source (including made in-house)
- stores/bin location (multi-location)
- unit of measure, eg sheets/square feet, bar/feet, etc
- re-order level, re-order quantity, min/max stock
- unit cost (provision for more than one)
- selling price where appropriate
- procurement lead time
- product code.

4. Recording of receipts, issues and physical inventory balance on each item.

5. The ability to accept input of data for goods received, and by reference to purchase or works order files, print a goods received note (GRN) with full details, eg purchase or works order number, GRN number, quantity, supplier advice note details, etc. Automatic allocation of GRN serial numbers.

6. Component issue by requisition or kitting list.

7. Automatic removal of picked quantities from 'allocated' status, and reduction of 'quantity on hand'.

8. Automatic updating of 'on order' quantities on raising purchase orders via the purchase order processing system.

9. Down-dating of 'on order' quantity on acceptance of materials from quality control, and not by raising GRNs.

10. 'In inspection' category in inventory file.

11. Printing of perpetual inventory listings.

12. ABC inventory analysis.

13. An audit trail maintained throughout the inventory control function.

14. A status report giving quantity on hand, on order, pre-allocated, allocated, in inspection.

15. An obsolete/slow moving inventory report, listing all items which have not been issued since a given date.

16. Material batch traceability.

17. Inventory evaluation report, as required.

18. Printing of stocktake sheets.

19. Trial kitting facility, with shortage lists where required.

20. Outstanding purchase/works orders report by part number.

3.6 Purchase order processing

The following features are required of the purchase order processing system:

1. Interfaces with the Inventory Control and Accounts Payable modules.

2. On-line additions, deletions, amendments or enquiries.

3. Automatic update of the 'on order' quantity in the inventory file.

4. The printing of purchase orders, either at the time of entry or later.

5. The ability to enter a purchase order for any standard or non-standard item for subsequent processing, receipt and invoice clearance.

6. Purchase order to remain on file as an 'open order' until taken off by the user.

7. The ability to search the open orders and history files for specific orders/items by vendor, items or purchase order number.

8. Due/overdue reports by vendor, showing order number, part

number, due delivery date, also available by screen enquiry.

9. Outstanding orders report, showing all orders on file. Also available by screen enquiry.

10. The facility to add free-format text to any item description or special instruction field.

11. Purchase history to be retained for 12 months.

12. The provision of vendor performance data.

13. The facility to handle goods inwards inspection procedures and consequent rejections or transfers into inventory.

14. The ability to hold up to three alternative vendors per part/material.

15. The system should facilitate:
– multiple items per purchase order
– multiple advice receipts per order
– blanket orders.

16. The identification of rejections against individual purchase orders.

3.6 Costing

The following features are required of the costing system:

1. Interfaces with Inventory Control, Purchase Order Processing and Production Control modules.

2. On-line additions, deletions, amendments and enquiries.

3. Re-costing facility.

4. Retrieval of previous job costs, using customer, job description/number, part number or work centre.

5. Accumulation of actual costs to each works order/job. Labour costs from actual times recorded for each operation; material costs from material bookings; sub-contract costs from vendor invoices.

6. 'Roll-up' of low level costs into higher levels, using the product structures.

7. Overhead rates can be applied to work centres or individual machines.

8. Facility for cost analysis:
   i) by product and by works order

- direct materials, with scrap costs
- indirect materials
- direct labour
- works overheads
- works cost, ie materials plus labour plus factory overheads
- administrative overheads
- total cost

ii) by both value and percentage.

9. Cost variance reports, by product, by works order, comparing actual against planned costs.

10. A work-in-progress valuation report.
11. Cost history facilities to allow comparisons with current costs or estimates.
12. A cost of sales analysis.
13. Recording and costing of non-productive time, eg machine breakdown.
14. Analysis of productive and non-productive time, by employee.
15. Scrap analysis by work centre, showing by job number and operation the quantity and labour value.

3.7 Capacity planning and scheduling

The following features are required of the capacity planning and scheduling system:
1. Interfaces with Inventory Control, Product Data Management and Costing modules.
2. On-line insertions, deletions, amendments and enquiries.
3. Scheduling of all works orders into the production schedule using data held in product data management (parts, BOM, routes, capacities) and inventory files (materials available, allocations, etc).
4. Production of updated work centre loading reports, shown in Gannt chart and tabular form. The current load/overload profile for each work centre, for both labour and machines.
5. Printing of work-to lists for each machine/work centre, showing the sequence in which operations should be carried out.
6. Back scheduling of orders from due date, giving a starting date and due date for each operation.
7. Forward scheduling from a given start date, to give start date and due date for each operation.
8. Ability to schedule/re-schedule jobs on a 'what-if' basis, without affecting live data, until the optimum solution has been chosen.
9. The ability to set a priority against each order for shop scheduling sequence.

3.8 Production control (work-in-progress)

The following features are required of the production control system:
1. Interfaces with the Costing and Capacity Planning modules.
2. On-line insertions, deletions, amendments and enquiries.
3. The printing of route cards, showing:
- works order/batch number
- part number and description
- quantity
- start and finish dates;
and for each operation
- operation number
- operation/inspection description

- tooling/gauges required
- work centre/machine
- setting time
- running(operation) time.

4. Progress of an order to be updated from the route cards, in terms of:
- quantity completed
- quantity scrapped
- time taken(set-up)
- time taken(operation)
- job completion.

5. The facility to collect costs of materials issued and labour hours taken, by work centre, for all works orders, and to transfer these to the Costing module.

6. Printing of works orders.

7. The facility to enquire upon works order status, with comparison between projected completion dates and due dates.

8. An arrears schedule of all jobs not completed within the specified time period.

9. Materials issues from a kit can be carried out in part or whole.

10. Facilitates inspection operations which may result in scrapping or rectification work.

11. Accomodates customer order amendments which can change the status of items in progress (or stores) and may result in rejection or rectification work.

3.9 Materials requirements planning (MRP)

The features required of the MRP system are as follows:

1. Interfaces with the bill of materials, master schedule, inventory control and sales order processing systems.

2. Take product and spare parts requirements data from the master schedule and translate them into gross requirements for raw materials, components and sub-assemblies, using the BOMs on file.

3. The netting down of gross requirements by checking against available inventory in the inventory control files.

4. The printing of a suggested orders report, including purchase orders for raw materials, bought-out and sub-contract items, and works orders for made-in components.

5. The ability to 'group' purchase order requests by preferred supplier.

6. The ability to classify all materials and components as either MRP or Re-order point.

7. The facility to carry out both 'nett change' and 'regenerative' processing.

8. The ability to apply batching rules, scrap allowances and safety stock parameters.

9. The facility for pegging of requirements through all product structure levels.

4. DATA VOLUMES

4.1 Sales order processing

Number of sales orders/month: 450
Number of customers: 500
Average number of items/order: 10
Average number of sales orders outstanding: 600
Average number of invoices/month: 500
Average number of lines/invoice: 10
Number of months invoice history to be held on file: 12

4.2 Inventory control

Number of transactions/month: 500
Number of inventory items: 3,000
Number of months transaction history required: 12

4.3 Production planning and control

Number of manufacturing routes: 200
Number of work centres: 10
Average number of ops/route: 5
Average number of works orders in progress: 50
Number of works orders raised/week: 50

4.4 Bills of material

Number of bills on file: 100
Average number of lines/bill: 15

4.5 Costing

Number of works orders in progress: 60
Number of cost centres: 8

4.6 Purchase order processing

Number of purchase orders/month: 100
Average number of lines/order: 5
Number of months purchase order history to be held on file: 12
Note: The above data volumes are an approximation. The sizing of the system, to determine hardware requirements, is the responsibility of the systems vendor.

5. HARDWARE REQUIREMENTS

5.1 General

The hardware supplied must be of proven reliability and be capable of on-site upgrades if necessary. It must be capable of operation by the existing staff at XYZ Co, and full support should be available from the vendor in terms of diagnostic facilities, 'hot-line' advice and a range of call-out options.

The hardware should be capable of operating in a normal office environment, and the various housekeeping routines (eg security copying) should be capable of operation by existing staff. The hardware must be fully supported by user manuals and guides.

5.2 Central processor

The central processing unit (CPU) should include the following features:

- ability to support up to 20 workstations and up to 5 printers
- fast security copying and archiving system
- does not require to be kept in an air-conditioned environment.

5.3 Terminal equipment

The terminal equipment required initially will be comprised of:

- 12 visual display units
- 3 dot matrix printers
- 1 letter-quality printer.

Note: The requirement for hardware, including CPU, VDUs and printers, will depend on the compatibility of the proposed hardware/software with the existing hardware.

Appendix II:

TENDER COSTS

VENDOR: *JONES SYSTEMS*	One-off Cost	Annual Cost
HARDWARE		
1 × CPU, Model ABC123, 2Mb memory	60,000	6,000
2 × 71Mb hard disks	8,000	800
1 × Magnetic tape streamer	2,000	200
10 × B65 workstations	20,000	2,000
1 × System console	2,000	200
3 × Dot-matrix printers	4,000	400
1 × NLQ printer	3,000	300
HARDWARE MAINTENANCE	——	9,900
DELIVERY	2,000	——
INSTALLATION (cabling, power supply, modems)	5,000	——
TRAINING	3,500	——
OPERATING SOFTWARE	2,500	250
APPLICATIONS SOFTWARE:		
Sales order processing	2,500	300
Inventory control	2,500	300
Purchase order control	2,000	240
Costing	2,000	240
Materials requirements planning (MRP)	3,000	360
Bill of material (BOM) and routeings	4,000	480
Works orders	2,000	240
Work-in-process	2,000	240
Production control	3,000	360
TOTALS	135,000	12,910

Appendix III: SUMMARY

VENDOR	COMPUTER	TERMINALS	OPERATING SOFTWARE	APPLICATIONS SOFTWARE	DELIVERY AND INSTALLATION	TRAINING AND IMPLEMENT- ATION	TOTAL CAPITAL COSTS	ANNUAL MAINTENANCE COST	ANNUAL COST OVER 5 YEARS
Jones System	70,000	29,000	2,500	23,000	7,000	3,500	135,000	12,910	29,582
Smith Computers	60,000	26,000	4,000	31,000	6,000	4,500	131,500	14,465	29,193
ACME Software	85,000	32,000	3,000	29,000	8,000	6,000	163,000	14,670	35,534
Production Systems	55,000	26,000	4,000	24,000	5,000	5,000	119,000	14,280	26,656

Appendix IV:
IMPLEMENTATION PLAN

Activities	Aug 25	1	8	15	22	29	Sep 5	12	19	26	Oct 3	10	17	24	31	Nov 7	14	21	28
PLANNING I																			
Reqs investigation	▆																		
Appoint steer comm								▪											
Implementation plan			▪▆																
Computer specification			▆▆																
Approve specification				▆▆															
Steering comm meeting									▪										
Submit inv to tender					▪														
Vet tenders											▆								
User visits												▆▆							
Steering comm meeting													▪						
Select system														▆					
Manual systems review														▆					
PREPARATION I																			
Data Check																			
BOM data														▆▆					
Pur order data														▆▆					
Supplier data														▆▆					
Inventory data									▆▆▆▆▆										
Decide document formats													▆						
Order stationery														▪					
Site survey														▪					
Steering comm meeting														▪					
DELIVERY & INSTALL																			
Site preparation																▪			
Cabling																▪			
Set-up																▪			
Hardware delivery																▪			
Software delivery																▪			
H'ware set-up/test																▪			
S'ware set-up/test																▪			
EDUCATION & TRAINING I																			
BOM																▪			
Inventory control																▪			
Purchase orders																▪			
Sales orders																▪			
DATA ENTRY I																			
Set-up																	▪		
System parameters																	▪		
Parts master files																	▪		
Supplier files																	▪		
Purchase order files																	▪		
BOM files																	▪		
Steering comm meeting																	▪		
Entry																			
Inventory data																		▆▆	
Supplier data																			
Purchase order data																			
BOM data																			
Sales order data																			
Trial running																			

Index